TALES FROM THE
SKY KITCHEN CAFE

TALES FROM THE

SKY
KITCHEN
CAFE

MIKE PAULL

Published by Skyhawk Publishing

Printed in the USA

Design by Carla Resnick

ISBN 978-0-615-44109-2

Library of Congress Catalog Number 2010919405

Dedication

To Bev, my wife of 50 years, who encouraged me to write this book. To our children Barrie and Jeff, who have brought us two beautiful boys. To the bonus of our life, our grandsons, Blake and Jamey.

A special thanks to

Bev Paull, Bonnie Paull, and Candyce Griswold for their constructive criticism, critical evaluation, and editing of the book.

Barrie Scheid and Deme Jamson for their creative inspiration.

"…….Flight is but momentary escape from the eternal custody of earth."

—Beryl Markham, 1936
Pioneer aviatrix

CONTENTS

Foreword

With the sad—and to pilots imponderable—decline of public interest in general aviation, this book appears at exactly the right time. The author goes to the very heart of aviation by illustrating the true pleasure to be found in flight.

This is a different sort of a book. Mike uses the backdrop of the Sky Kitchen Cafe, where his subjects met everyday, to illustrate through words, the friendship and brotherhood between the men and women in his stories. He weaves this theme throughout all the emotion-filled stories in his book. Best of all, Mike's passion for flying and friendship comes through loud and clear.

My background as a military pilot made the story titled *The Pilot and the POW* especially compelling. In it, Mike tells the story of two World War II aviators who meet at the cafe fifty years after the war, and find that they shared a common day in history. The story describes the cruelty of war and, more important, the ability of man to survive.

The author has successfully written a series of aviation based stories in a language which allows readers with no background in the subject to understand and enjoy them.

The book is a first of its kind. I wish Mike had written it earlier, and I hope he writes another...

Walter J. Boyne
Author/Historian
Former Director, National Air and Space Museum
Inducted into Aviation Hall of Fame, 2007

Prologue

A DAY TO REMEMBER

Tales from the Sky Kitchen Cafe

A DAY TO REMEMBER

August 25, 1978 didn't appear to be anything other than an ordinary summer day in the San Francisco Bay Area. Most people would never recall it, but for me it turned out to be one I would remember for the rest of my life. It was the day I embarked on an adventure, which became my life's passion, a journey that thirty-two years later excites me as much as it did then.

By 1978 I had been practicing dentistry for fifteen years. Four days a week I went to my office in San Carlos, California to treat patients, some of whom I had seen since they were youngsters. That August day Jim, a young guy in his twenties, and a patient since he was a teenager, flopped down in the dental chair and asked, *"Hey, Doc, how would you like a free flying lesson?"*

Jim, who had already earned a college degree in engineering, decided he wanted a more exciting profession. He chose aviation. In his quest to be an airline pilot, he was at the flight instructor stage. In order to build hours and experience a flight instructor recruits students to provide a meager living and to pay for the flight time that he desperately needs to move up to the next level.

"A what?" I said.

"A free flight lesson" Jim said again. *"I work for a flight school. They have planes available. We can go up tonight and there's no charge; I'll even give you a logbook to record your first flight."*

I was the ideal candidate for flying lessons. I was thirty-nine years old, only three months short of what most consider the entrance to middle age. I loved dentistry, but the work was intense and very confining. The only cockpit I ever navigated was a ten by twelve treatment room, and the closest I came to the clouds was a glimpse of them through my window.

My excitement had me watching the clock until six o'clock finally rolled around. That was the time I met Jim at the local airport. We spent a few minutes talking about the basics and then I climbed into the left seat of the smallest plane on the ramp, a Cessna 152. Jim jumped into the right seat next to me and we taxied out to the runway. We flew for about a half hour. Jim did most of the flying, but he allowed me to think that I was in control. After the flight, we sat and had a cup of coffee. *"You're a natural,"* Jim said. I found out later it was a line from the Flight Instructor's Sales Manual; but it wouldn't have mattered if I had known it then. Jim baited the hook, I swallowed it, and it has been lodged in my gut for thirty-two years.

It took about six months to earn my first license, Private Pilot. It turned out instead to be a license to learn. I was authorized to be the Pilot in Command of an aircraft; and it was an awesome feeling, but also an awesome responsibility. To meet that responsibility I, like thousands of pilots before me, continued to train and earn additional licenses and specialized ratings. The more I learned, the more I realized how much was left to learn.

I soon found there was a community of pilots who loved to talk about flying. Once the discussions got started, it was almost as exciting as flying itself. We congregated either in hangars, out on the Tarmac, or in the parking lot to talk about flying. Our favorite gathering place, however, was the restaurant located at the airport called the Sky Kitchen Cafe.

The Sky Kitchen is located in the terminal building next to the airport office and a small pilot supply store. It is a combination of coffee shop and diner, and is only open for breakfast and lunch. It has a half dozen tables located next to the windows, so that patrons can watch the airplanes take off and land. It also has a counter near the kitchen, where the customers smell bacon cooking and hear coffee perking. This counter is cozy, but that's not where the local pilots sit. In the center of the room there's a counter, formed in the shape of a loose circle, which accommodates about a dozen people. During the lunch hour pilots jockey for a seat. Once seated, the regulars can carry on conversations with almost anyone at the counter. It's rare that a non-pilot finds his way to the center counter, however, if he does, he soon finds he is surrounded by members of a fraternity; not a formal fraternity as one would find at a college or university, but an informal one, whose members are bonded together by common flight experiences and a common love for flying.

Fraternities at colleges attract members near the same age, who are going through the same period of the life cycle and who, after four or five years get on with their lives. The fraternity that meets at the Sky Kitchen every day at lunchtime is very, very different. The age of the pilots vary from kids as young as seventeen, to veterans of civil and military aviation, some of whom are in their late eighties. Their flight experience also varies tremendously. Some are student pilots with ten or twenty hours in the cockpit, while others are airline pilots with twenty or thirty thousand hours. The most incredible difference, however, is the backgrounds and vocations of the members. On any given day at the Sky Kitchen, one can find a plumber, an electrician, a physician, an accountant, a dentist, or a highway patrolman seated at the counter. There are also computer geeks and computer salesmen. There are airline pilots and airplane mechanics. There are house builders and housewives. Some are exceedingly successful financially and others are struggling to save enough money to fill the gas tank for their next flight. A fraternity based on a shared passion.

It was there, at the center counter of the Sky Kitchen Cafe, where I spent almost every one of my lunch hours for twenty years. It was there where I made lifelong friends, who shared their experiences with me, and whose stories I now share with you, in the *Tales from the Sky Kitchen Cafe*.

LEN GIVES ME A SCARE

Tales from the Sky Kitchen Cafe

Len Gives Me a Scare

The first thing a new pilot does, when he gets his license, is take all his friends up in the air to display his new skills. My best friend was Len, another dentist who practiced nearby. He was the first of my friends to get an invitation to ride in the used Cessna 172 I had purchased. It had four seats, two more than the 152 in which I had trained. Len loved both the plane and the ride so much, that we made plans to take a trip with our wives to Sunriver, Oregon, about three and a half hours north. The trip did not exactly go smoothly. I was new to navigation and couldn't locate the airport immediately, which extended the trip by an extra half hour. It was a very hot day and when we flew over the high terrain in Central Oregon, the hot air rising off the ground created a constant turbulence. Len was riding in the back seat and was doing his best to hold down his lunch. The extra half hour was too much for him. Not being able to locate an airsick bag, he used the nearest container he could find; He pulled off his shoe.

Three days later when we piled into the plane for the trip home, I found that I had left the master switch on for the entire stay. The battery was completely dead, and we had to wait for a truck to come and jump it. We obviously got a late start for home and of course, encountered rising hot air, and of course, more turbulence. Len was better because he had chosen not to eat before we left. I was positive Len was through with flying and would never try it again. To my surprise he said, *"That was fun; how do I get a license?"*

The Cessna 172 which I had purchased was a 1975 model. Four years of previous use is not much for an airplane. Very few people purchase new planes because of the prohibitive cost. Many airplanes in the general aviation fleet today are twenty, thirty or forty years old. Airplanes have mandatory maintenance requirements; it is not unusual to see an airplane that is a quarter century old, looking and operating as if it had just come off the assembly line at the factory. The 172 was a nice running, average looking plane. Based on automobile comparisons, it would have been considered a compact Chevrolet as opposed to a big Cadillac.

When Len expressed interest in flying, I had a bright idea. Instead of Len having to rent a trainer, I would sell him a fifty percent interest in the 172. He would have a plane in which to train as well as one to fly after he received his license. I would have a partner who would absorb fifty percent of the maintenance costs. The idea excited Len and soon we were partners.

Len wanted to begin his training in the 172; the only thing missing was a flight instructor. Len knew my instructor Jim, and I suggested he contact him. They got together, related well to each other, and soon Len was into his flight training.

Part of the flight training in preparation for a license requires what is called Cross Country Flights. This is not a literal description, because in this context it means legs of twenty-five to one hundred miles between airports. There are three airports in the sequence with a landing at each one. To prepare for a license the candidate is required to make three solo cross country flights. The first one is usually the shortest, the last one the longest. It was the 30th of March and Len was getting ready to make his first solo cross country trip. He and Jim went over the route, the airports, the runways, the navigation and the weather. When Len departed around noon on his first leg, the winds were calm and not forecasted to increase significantly.

I was working in my office and around 3 o'clock I glanced out the window. The trees branches were swaying and the wind was kicking up. I felt a little twinge in the pit of my stomach, but went back to work. Around 4 o'clock I received a phone call that turned the twinge into a knot. *"This is the control tower at San Carlos Airport. Are you the owner of a Cessna 172 number N80362?"*

"I'm one of the owners," I answered.

"Can you get down here? There's been an accident," the controller replied.

I froze. I stammered, *"Is anyone hurt?"*

"I can't give you that information on the phone. Can you get down here?"

I jumped into my car and raced toward the airport. As I approached an ambulance was speeding in the opposite direction. I pulled into the airport and could see several emergency lights near the dyke which holds the bay water from flooding the airport. When I reached the lights, my heart almost stopped. There in the water with only its tail sticking out, sat the 172. I quickly extracted enough information to determine that Len was not seriously hurt, but was taken to the hospital for observation. I made the call to his wife, and met her at the hospital. I had a weight lifted from my shoulders, when the doctor confirmed that Len was fine.

It seems that my trepidation over the wind was justified. The velocity had slowly increased since noon, when Len had departed, and by the time he returned a strong cross wind had developed. As a beginning student he was taught basic crosswind landing techniques, but it takes a great deal of experience to handle them, when they approach an 80 to 90 degree angle to the runway—that was exactly the situation, when Len attempted to land.

Len later related the incident to me. *"After three attempts to land and not being able to get close to the runway, the fourth attempt looked like it would work; however, as I relaxed the controls, a huge gust raised my left wing and I thought for sure I was going to scrape the wing on the runway. I gave it full power again, but really didn't have control of the airplane as I turned toward the bay. My airspeed got low and as I turned near the dyke, the right wing caught the top of it. The airplane did a 180 degree tip over into the water. I hit my tough Sicilian head on the control panel breaking one of the gauges. Fortunately, I didn't pass out or I would have drowned in the cockpit. I climbed out and held onto the tail of the plane, the only part not submerged. I stayed there until the rescue crew brought me ashore."*

The next day I asked Len, if he was concerned that the plane would sink. He responded, *"I wasn't really scared until the channel 5 news helicopter flew overhead and damn near drowned me with the water it kicked up over the tail."*

Len and I went to see the airplane. It had been lifted out of the water and was declared totaled by the insurance company. I wanted to save something from the airplane. Sitting on the luggage shelf in the back of the airplane was a stuffed animal my wife had given me for good luck. It was the Snoopy character from the "Peanuts" comic strip. He was dressed to look like the WWI ace, Red Baron. He had a leather flight jacket, scarf, helmet and goggles and he was no worse for wear after his experience. He just sat there smiling at me. I took

Snoopy with me, and although I'm not a superstitious person, I have placed him in the back of the six airplanes I have owned since the 172. He sits today on the luggage shelf in the back of a sleek Bonanza F33, and is still smiling as he did thirty years ago.

I was concerned for Len. He had gone through a traumatic experience and to compound it, he felt guilty for losing the airplane. I did my best trying to convince him that it was a hunk of metal and could be replaced; but I'm not sure he ever bought it. It was a difficult day, when Len returned for the first time to the Sky Kitchen. He was embarrassed and hoped the other pilots at the counter would understand. Part of being a pilot is reading about accidents and trying to learn from the mistakes of others. They all know that even an experienced pilot can be the subject of the next accident report. Everyone at the center counter greeted Len warmly, slapped him on the back and did his best to let Len know that it was alright. He received support, encouragement, and even praise from the members of the fraternity at the center counter.

To his credit, Len earned his pilot license about six months later. He turned out to be one of the safest, most conscientious pilots with whom I have ever flown. We bought a beautiful six seat Bonanza A36 together with another dentist/pilot two years later. We flew hundreds of hours together including trips to Mexico and the Bahamas. Len has flown over two thousand hours since that first cross country flight, and has never had an event that even resembled a close call. His flying record stands unblemished, since that fateful day in March.

RESCUED

Ron Alvis, a Medevac technician, and Jim Ahern are able to secure a line to pilot Dr. Leonard Vinci in a successful rescue attempt Monday afternoon near San Carlos Airport.

Wind whips airplane into slough at San Carlos Airport

A 46-year-old Belmont dentist, flying on his maiden cross-country solo flight, crashed into a slough just east of the San Carlos Airport Monday afternoon when his single-engine Cessna 172 became caught in strong gusts of cross winds, causing a wing tip to strike a levee, San Carlos police reported.

Taken to Sequoia Hospital for a checkup after he was brought to land from the three-quarters submerged plane was Dr. Leonard A. Vinci of 1095 Palomar Drive, Redwood City, who has his practice at 2120 Carlmont Drive, Belmont.

According to Lt. Clifford Gerst, Vinci climbed out of the plane with only a minor head abrasion. Officers said Medevac attendant Ron Alvis took a line from shore out to the plane. Jim Ahern, a swimming coach at Serramonte High School, who was at the airport at the time of the crash, volunteered to take out a second line to help Vinci to shore.

A helicopter from TV station KPIX, hovering overhead, dropped a life jacket to Vinci.

According to Gerst, the control tower operator reported that winds from the northwest were blowing at about 20 knots and gusting up to 30 knots at the time of the crash.

Vinci told rescuers he had made several passes at the runway and apparently stalled out as he attempted to pull up again after deciding to abort his landing.

Firemen said that the plane crashed into Steinberger Slough about 100 yards off shore. Vinci was clinging to the tail of the plane 15 to 20 minutes before being hauled to shore, police said. They reported the plane was badly damaged.

Prime rate up to 19¾ pct.

NEW YORK (UPI) — Chase Manhattan, the nation's third largest bank, Tuesday raised its prime lending rate to a record 19¾ percent from 19¼ percent. The prevailing rate is 19½ percent.

Earlier in the day Citibank of New York, normally a trendsetter, boosted the rate it charges its most creditworthy corporate customers to 19½ percent from 19¼. First National Bank of Chicago took a similar step Monday.

Banks have raised this key rate because the Federal Reserve has tightened and restricted credit, forcing interest rates sharply higher. Many analysts predict the prime rate will rise above 20 percent soon.

Headlines April 1, 1980

Len being rescued from the tail of the 172

Mike (left), Len (right), on a trip to Mexico, four years after the accident

Snoopy, still smiling after thirty years

A Mentor's Mentor

Tales from the Sky Kitchen Cafe

A Mentor's Mentor

Every pilot has had at least one mentor and some have had many. Webster's defines mentor as a trusted counselor, guide, tutor or coach.

Jim was my original flight instructor, and by default became my mentor. After I earned my pilot license he was the guy I'd call, when I needed help with a flight, a procedure, or a piece of equipment. Even years after he had moved on in his career, I'd track him down with an aviation problem or question; most of the time he had the answer. It never occurred to me that as he progressed up the aviation ladder, he also would need a mentor.

After three years working as a flight instructor, Jim was hired by a commuter airline based in Yuma, Arizona. It didn't pay much, but it was the stepping stone to a major airline job. The airline industry was on the upswing and in 1982 Jim interviewed with Northwest Airlines, a company that was expanding rapidly. He was hired and soon found himself working the right (co-pilot) seat on domestic flights.

Pilots were allowed to bid for the planes and the routes they wanted to fly. The assignments were given out on the basis of the pilot's seniority number. In 1986 Jim realized Northwest had hired so many pilots in the past four years, that he possessed a very low number. He decided to take a shot and make a bid to fly in the co-pilot seat of the biggest wide-body aircraft in the sky, a Boeing 747-200. For Jim dreams did come true. In eight years he had gone from flying a two seat 1,600 lb. airplane across San Francisco bay, to flying a three hundred fifty seat 833,000 lb. airplane across the Pacific Ocean.

Jim checked the schedule and found his name as first officer (co-pilot) of flight #7 from Seattle's Seatac Airport to Tokyo's Narita International.

He entered the flight operations room and spotted his captain for the flight, an experienced guy named Jens, who had a reputation as one of the most respected among the Northwest pilots.

Jim's nerves were working overtime as the pilots went through their pre-flight. Once the four engines got started he began to relax and settle into his job for the flight. The captain flew the entire leg while Jim ran the radios and performed the navigation. Ten hours and eight minutes later, Jens greased the wheels onto Narita's runway, taxied to the gate, and shut down the engines. Seated on the bus for the ride to the hotel, Jim replayed the flight in his head. *"Wow the captain made that look easy. I think I'm going to learn something from this guy; can't wait to see how he handles tomorrow's leg to Hong Kong."*

Planning for the flight to Kai Tak airport started a couple hours before departure time. Other than the captain, only the first officer was allowed into the flight planning room. Jim thought he might pop the chest buttons of his shirt as he accompanied Jens into the planning session, while the other two officers kept walking to the plane to ready it for departure.

It was going to be a night arrival in Hong Kong and the weather report was calling for stormy conditions. Rain, gusty winds and a slick runway were going to make this an "interesting" approach and landing. The airport is right in the middle of downtown and the instrument procedure used by the pilots is one of the trickiest and well known in the world. It's called the Cheung Chau Checkerboard IGS to Runway 13. Jim thought, *"This arrival is not for the weak of heart. I'm glad I'm with Jens on this one. It's still five hours away, but I can't wait to see how a pro like him handles it."*

Jim followed the captain into the cockpit and started to decipher the briefing, arrange the charts and set the radios. Although Jim was looking forward to the arrival in Hong Kong, the departure out of Tokyo was not going to be a piece of cake. It was dark, raining, and there was a gusty crosswind blowing across the runway. Even the taxi from the ramp to the runway was getting Jim's attention.

The tower controller's directions came over the radio. *"Line up and wait"*.

Jim was working the radios and acknowledged, *"Line up and wait, Northwest 17"*.

Jens eased the huge plane into position on the centerline of the runway.

"Northwest 17 cleared for takeoff."

Jim echoed back, "Northwest 17, cleared to go."

Jim settled back in his chair and waited for Jens to advance the throttles, instead the captain just sat quietly in his seat. Jim looked over at Jens. Jens looked back at Jim and said, *"Well are we going or not?"* It took a few seconds before Jim realized that the captain was letting him fly the leg from Narita to Kai Tak.

Jim had only flown the 747 three times before tonight and it was always in calm, daylight conditions. He advanced the throttles, configured the plane for the crosswind, and within thirty seconds was flying three hundred and eighty-five people to China. After leveling off at 32,000 ft., Jim started to pay attention to the second officer's reports regarding weather and altitudes which might avoid turbulence. Jim looked over at Jens, waiting for a suggestion. Looking nonchalant, Jens said, *"You're the guy flying, do what you want, but I still get the first choice of the dinners."*

The flight was calculated to take four hours and thirteen minutes. Jim crossed over the island of Taiwan; knowing there was only an hour remaining, before they reached Hong Kong, he started planning his descent. As they got closer he said to himself, *"Oh, what the hell, we're 130 miles from Hong Kong; I think this is the right spot to descend. I hope he doesn't disagree too much."* Jens didn't say a word and continued to wipe his glasses with a Kleenex.

On any airplane large or small speed control is always an issue as the airport draws near. Jim was getting close to the final approach course and the plane was still carrying a speed of 240 knots (276 mph). Jens quietly suggested, *"One degree of flaps might be a good idea."*

"Flaps one" Jim barked. A few minutes later, *"flaps five"*, followed by *"flaps ten"*.

The 747 started to slow up as Jim intercepted the famous Checkerboard IGS instrument approach course. Jens very slowly moved his hand toward the landing gear handle. Jim saw it out of the corner of his eye.

"Gear down, flaps 20", Jim ordered. Jens responded and lowered the landing gear; the speed was under control.

Jim was concentrating on keeping his instrument needles centered so that he was in perfect line with the runway. Mother Nature was trying her best to disrupt him. It was raining cats and dogs, the gusts were hammering the plane, and there was a tailwind that forced it across the ground faster than expected. Jim called out *"flaps 25, landing check."*

Kai Tek does not offer a long runway for planes as large as a 747. Jim was working hard to touch down as soon as possible, but the runway was disappearing quickly behind him. Jim started to pull the control wheel toward him, raising the nose of the plane up, causing it to float above the runway. Without saying a word Jens put his thumb right in back of the control wheel preventing it from coming back any further. This disrupted the floating and the plane thumped hard on the blacktop without using up valuable runway. It wasn't the most graceful landing, but with Jens gentle guidance it was safe and it was over.

By the time the crew boarded the bus to the hotel Jim's adrenaline had finally begun to subside. As they stepped off the bus, Jens put his hand on Jim's shoulder and like a father after his son's little league game said, *"Good job Jim."*

Jim at work

Jim at play

THE PILOT AND THE POW

Tales from the Sky Kitchen Cafe

The Pilot and the POW

On March 10, 1945 the American Army Air Corps bombed and burned the center of Tokyo, Japan, creating a firestorm like none ever seen by man. There were two comrades who will never forget that day. They did not meet then because they were separated by one mile of sky. Fifty years later, in 1995, they met for the first time at the Sky Kitchen Cafe. Phil and Hap shared their incredible stories with each other and with the rest of us at the center counter. The two stories are quite different, but also very similar, because both men suffered the emotional wounds that war inflicts. Some of the wounds healed and left scars in their place. Others only created scabs, which were often torn off, leaving the wound open and exposed to pain once again.

Before the middle of 1944, the major bomber used by the United States was the B17, nicknamed the Flying Fortress. In May, 1944 the B29 Superfortress was introduced, primarily to be used in the Pacific Theatre against Japan. Like its predecessor, it had four engines and a crew of eleven, however, the B29 was equipped with major advancements over the B17.

The Superfortress had the capability to fly as high as 40,000 feet, higher than most enemy fighters could fly and beyond the range of most anti-aircraft weapons. The cabin was pressurized, reducing the crew members need to constantly breathe oxygen through masks. There was heat to protect the crew against the outside air temperatures, which often reached over fifty degrees below zero. It had a revolutionary control system for the four gunners, which included remote control turrets, an advanced analog computer that made corrections for airspeeds, gravity, temperature, barrel wear and humidity. The B29 was state of the art.

By the middle of 1944, the U.S. Marines had fought and taken control of most of the strategic islands that lay between Hawaii and Japan. Three thousand miles west of Honolulu sits a group of islands known as the Northern Marianas. On the three major islands in the group, the Americans built five large airstrips to accommodate use of the new state of the art bomber, the B29. One was on the island of Saipan, one on the island of Guam, and three on the island of Tinian. From these islands, hundreds of B29's made the fifteen hundred mile trip north to Japan, dropped their bombs, and made the fifteen hundred mile trip back to the Marianas. Normally, the planes were in the air for at least fifteen hours, but often hits from the enemy caused the loss of fuel or crippled engines, and they were forced to make emergency landings on the island of Iwo Jima, halfway between Saipan and Japan.

In 1943 Phil was twenty-two years old. Names like Saipan, Iwo Jima and Tokyo, were places that newspapers talked about, but were so far away that to him they only represented dots on a map. In the later part of 1943 Phil received a letter from the War Department informing him to report for induction. He knew he didn't want to be a ground soldier, so he applied and was accepted into the Army Air Corps cadet program. Phil's initial training for single engine aircraft was in Visalia, California. After a stop in Lancaster, California, he went on to Marfa,

Texas for twin engine training and finally to Salt Lake City, Utah, where he was trained to fly the B17.

In preparation for combat in Europe, Phil went to Great Bend, Kansas and then was assigned to an actual B17 crew in Roswell, New Mexico. Within eight short months, twenty-two year old Phil had gone from never having been in an airplane, to occupying the right co-pilot seat in a B17 bomber. As he was preparing to depart for Europe, his commander came to him and said, *"We need pilots for the new B29's, can we count on you?"*

"Sure, I'll do it," Phil replied, and soon he became a co-pilot on a Superfortress. Before long, the newly trained pilots boarded a commercial airliner and were flown not to Europe, but to Saipan.

Phil and the other new pilots arrived on Saipan November 1st, 1944, the same day the first B29 flew over Tokyo at 35,000 ft. on a reconnaissance flight. They were assigned to Quonset huts each housing twenty men, segregated according to their training. The pilots had their own twenty man huts, as did the navigators, engineers and bombardiers.

A very somber atmosphere prevailed among the pilots on Saipan. One of the pilots in Phil's hut created a mortality list. Every time one of the original twenty failed to return from a mission, his name was crossed off the list. New pilots were brought from the States to fill the empty cots, but in the eight months Phil spent on Saipan, only he and three other of the original twenty pilots still occupied the hut.

Because the mortality rate was so high, most of the pilots were cautious about making close friendships. They kept their distance from one another to shelter themselves against the pain inflicted when a comrade didn't return from a mission. Too many times a pilot would take a jeep to the end of the runway to wait for the returning planes. If twenty hours had passed since the beginning of the mission and a buddy's plane was not back, there was no hope that it would return. Some reports followed that confirmed which planes were shot down or had landed on Iwo Jima; the others were assumed to have run out of gas and were ditched into the sea.

Once on Saipan no time was wasted getting the pilots into combat. Phil was assigned to the co-pilot seat of a B29. On Thanksgiving Day, November 24th 1944, Phil made his first combat mission. The destination was Tokyo. It was also historic, because it was the very first of many combat missions the air force would fly over Japan from the Marianas. One hundred and eleven planes dropped their bombs from over 30,000 ft. above Tokyo. At those altitudes they were, for the most part, separated from the enemy's fighters and flak, keeping casualties to a minimum. After flying six missions in the right co-pilot seat, Phil was promoted to the left seat as an Aircraft Commander. It was December 1944 and he had earned his own B29, along with a crew. The name was already painted on the side of the plane. It was called Sentimental Journey

Like the other pilots stationed on Saipan, Phil had avoided getting too close to the other pilots, but for Johnnie he made an exception. They became friends before arriving on the island. Phil had met Johnnie when they were training in Grand Bend, Kansas. Johnnie had a three year old son, who had developed a collapsed lung and needed immediate transport from Grand Bend, Kansas to Chicago, Illinois. Phil managed to get use of a B17 and ferried Johnnie, his wife, his ailing son and a flight surgeon to Chicago, where an ambulance from Childrens Hospital was waiting. Phil stayed with the B17 until the ambulance brought the foursome back to the plane following a successful operation. Phil fired up the four engines and they headed back to Kansas.

Phil and Johnnie had arrived on Saipan together and short-ly thereafter, both had received command of B29's. Tokyo was one of the main targets of the bombing missions from Saipan and both men were preparing mentally for the next mis-sion. After every mission more names were being crossed off the mortality list in the Quonset hut. Phil and Johnnie went fishing, killing time the day before the next mission. Johnnie said, *"Phil, will you fly on my wing tomorrow in the formation?"*

"Sure, I'd be glad to," Phil replied. That mission created one of the emotional wounds that never healed for Phil. He can talk about it, but only with tears rolling down his cheeks.

The next day, the B29's established their formation and set off on the fifteen hour mission to Tokyo. The target was #357, the Nakajima Aircraft plant on the west side of Tokyo. As promised Phil's wing and Johnnie's wing were side by side at 30,000 ft. As the formation approached Mt. Fuji-yama, Japanese fighters appeared in the sky. One of them aimed his plane directly at Phil and Johnnie. There was no way of avoiding the Kamikaze suicide fighter. As it rammed itself into the side of Johnnie's B29, Phil could see the copilot sliced in half and could see a smile on the face of the Japa-nese pilot. Metal flew everywhere as Phil maneuvered his B29 away from the debris. Johnnie's plane was seriously damaged, especially on the right side where the fighter's wing tore into it. The 120,000 lb. aircraft was losing altitude and Johnnie was trying desperately to maintain control.

Phil broke from the formation in hope of attracting the other fighters toward his plane. It didn't help. Two other Kamikaze fighters, smelling the blood of their wounded prey, rammed the B29, while they blew themselves to smith-ereens. Johnnie's plane was mortally wounded and spinning toward the water below. Phil followed him down until he could go no farther and then applied full power to get his plane and crew back to the safety of the formation. Phil never got over that experience of watching his best friend disappear into the ocean.

Sixty years later while viewing Fifi, the last B29 still flying from the fleet of 3,970 built, Phil met a former tail gunner who told him he spent the end of the war in a Japanese prison camp after bailing out of a B29. Phil was again brought to tears when he learned the man was Johnnie's tail gunner. It turned out three men were able to bail out of that plane before it hit the water. Johnnie was not one of them.

The relative safety of high altitude bombing, 30,000 ft. and above soon changed. Although their high altitude provided some protection for the bombers, it also decreased the accuracy and the impact of their bomb runs. General Curtis Lemay, the newly appointed commander of the American Bomber Command, ordered a dramatic change in tactics. The high altitude daylight bombing would be replaced with low altitude nighttime missions. The planes would deliver a mixture of high explosive and incendiary (fire producing) bombs. He also ordered the removal of most of the defensive armament and remote controlled sighting equipment, so that the B29's could carry greater fuel and bomb loads. The new tactics improved the effectiveness of the bombing runs, but it also increased the loss of B29's and their crews. The low altitudes exposed them to enemy fighters and to anti-aircraft fire from the ground.

As the low level bombing continued, the number and intensity of the missions increased. During one four day period, Phil and his crew made five roundtrip bombing runs to Tokyo and back, stopping only for fuel, bombs and armaments each time they returned to Saipan. With each run taking at least fifteen hours, the crews were in the air for over seventy-five hours, sneaking sleep while the engines were droning away. Although Phil earned the Distinguished Flying Cross for the missions, the award left a hollow feeling, because every mission flown resulted in planes going down, leaving more empty cots in the huts the next night.

The memories of those flights are buried deep in Phil's subconscious, and when he talks of them, wounds are re-opened and visions come exploding to the surface: *"All of a sudden, I see myself dodging that guy, he's going down, that other guy just hit the water, I'm dodging bodies, that other plane landed on the water, guys crawling out of the airplane, hands reaching up and calling me to come down and help them but I can't do it; we let our life rafts out and that's all we can do. We say goodbye and leave them to die, some of them might make it but I wonder how."*

In 1945 the turning point of the war against Japan was about to take place. The Allies had first encountered the phenomenon of the firestorm, when the British bombed the German city of Hamburg in August 1943. The night raid ignited numerous fires that soon united into one uncontrol-lable mass of flame, so hot it generated its own self-sustaining gale-force winds and literally sucked oxygen out of the air, suf-focating its victims. General Lemay hoped to use this force to level the cities of Japan. Tokyo would be the first test. A suc-cessful incendiary raid required ideal weather which included dry air and significant wind. Weather reports predicted these conditions over Tokyo on the nights of March 9-10, 1945.

Phil had been designated as the Pathfinder on his previ-ous missions. The Pathfinder was the first plane to reach the destination, locate the target and drop incendiary bombs on it. The fire set by his bombs would mark the target for the rest of the bombers on the mission. The briefing for the mission of March 9th was no different than the previous ones. Phil and his crew were shown the primary target on the maps, and it would be their task to locate it and drop their bombs in the shape of a cross. The cross would act as a marker for the planes following the Pathfinder, giving them a target for their bomb drops. The pilots had no reason to believe that this mission was any different than any other they had flown over Tokyo. Nobody told them what destruction was planned for Tokyo that night. It wasn't their job to know. Their job was to find the target and bomb it.

Over one hundred B29's had been readied for combat on the island of Saipan. Each plane was stripped of ammunition for its machine guns to allow them to carry more firebombs. Phil and the other pilots had no idea that over two hundred more Superfortresses were also readied on the islands of Guam and Tinian. Around 7 p.m. on March 9, 1945, the formation departed Saipan, following their Pathfinder toward Tokyo.

The bombers' primary target was the industrial district of the city that neighbored factories, docks, and the homes of workers who supplied manpower for Japan's industry. The district hugged Tokyo Bay and was densely-packed with wooden homes lining winding streets that followed random paths – all the ingredients necessary for creating a perfect firestorm.

Seven hours after departing Saipan, around 1:30 a.m., Phil's navigator located the primary target in the industrial district of Tokyo. Three passes were made over the target at 5000 ft., each time dropping incendiary bombs that created a cross of fire on the ground. Phil's B29, Sentimental Journey, had just dropped the first bombs that would lead to the largest fire ever known to man. Over 100,000 people would burn to death in the next twenty-four hours, a higher death toll than that produced by the dropping of the atomic bomb on Hiroshima or

Nagasaki six months later.

When Phil pushed the throttles forward to execute his climb out, he could see the formation approaching from the south; in they came, dropping bomb after bomb on the target that was marked on the ground. The firestorm was under way and could be seen from over a hundred and fifty miles out. The Saipan raiders were already on their way home, when the planes from Guam and Tinian came in to add their bombs to the firestorm. A total of three hundred thirty-four B29's dropped bombs on Tokyo into the early hours of March 10th.

The fire burned all night and most of the next day. A total of seventeen square miles, an area almost half the size of San Francisco, was incinerated.

⸺⸺⸺

As his fellow B29 crews flew overhead just 5000 ft. above him, an American B29 navigator huddled in his cell, terrified he would die that night in a Japanese prison camp. The navigator, Hap, survived that night, survived the war and fifty years later wandered into the Sky Kitchen for lunch. He sat at the center counter and coincidentally sat next to a guy named Phil, the Pathfinder of the March 10th raid over Tokyo.

On December 7th 1941 the Japanese bombed Pearl Harbor. Hap was nineteen years old and living in Cincinnati, Ohio with his family. When the news was broadcast over the radio, Hap was with his father.

"Dad, this is terribly wrong. I want to help. I have to join up." His dad just nodded his head in agreement. Hap made his way to Wright Patterson field in Dayton and enlisted in the Army Air Corps. The Air Corps had a shortage of planes, bases and instructors in 1941, so Hap was sent home until late

1942, when he was finally called to active duty. All of the new recruits were given a series of tests to determine for which job they would be trained. Hap passed the tests for pilot, navigator and bombardier. He loved navigation and decided to take the training to become a navigator.

Between December 1942 and December 1944, Hap went through basic training, navigation training and bombardier training. They were told that the Air Corps was coming out with a new long range plane and wanted dual rated navigator/bombardiers. They weren't told the name of the plane or where it would be flown. It turned out to be the B29 and it would be used in the Pacific Theatre against Japan.

For Hap, the war was getting closer. He was sent to Smoky Hill Air Force Base in Salina, Kansas, where he joined ten other guys, forming a B29 crew of eleven. It took about a month or two for the crew to get to know each other. When the crew started to feel close to one another, they chose a name for themselves; The Rover Boys Express. They also chose nicknames for every member. Up until that time Hap had been known by his given name, Ray. The crew pinned the name Hap on him because he had a great sense of humor and always had a smile on his face. From that day on, Hap has been the only name he has used.

B29's were still scarce, so for the next eight or nine months the crew trained in B17's and B26's until finally they were able to get into a B29. They only had about sixty hours in B29's, when their time came to go to war. The crew was given a B29 and a brown envelope. The envelope told them to proceed to Mather Field in Sacramento, California. There they refueled and were given another brown envelope with instructions to proceed to Hawaii; another envelope sent them to Kwajalein in the Marshall Islands and the last envelope sent them to Saipan in the Northern Marianas. They arrived December 21, 1944.

When Quonset huts were assigned, the Rover Boys were split into two groups. The five officers, (two pilots, navigator, bombardier, engineer), were assigned to the same barracks. The four gunners, radar operator and radio operator were assigned to quarters at the other end of the base. Hap's crew was very close to each other, but the longevity of fliers was short and they had no desire to mingle with other crews in their hut. One crew was shot down before Hap could even remember their names.

Before his crew went on its first combat mission together, Hap flew one with another crew over Kobe, Japan. Hap was there to learn the navigation techniques which he would use to guide the Rover Boys Express to Tokyo. The crew was excited and ready to get into combat. They soon got their chance and flew two successful combat missions over Tokyo.

Their third mission was on Jan. 27th 1945. The target was #357, the Nakajima Aircraft plant; the same target that Phil's friend Johnnie was lost to a month earlier. The briefing was optimistic, *"Very few fighters at your altitude, very light flak if any at your altitude, have a good mission and we'll see you when you get back."* At 3 p.m., the Rover Boys Express was shot down over Tokyo.

As their airplane approached Tokyo in a loose formation at 31,000 ft., Japanese fighters were all over the sky. Hap remembers seeing at least fifty of them before making a 270 degree turn to locate their target. Several fighters came in below the B29 using guns that shot in an upward direction. *"We were hit in the nose, there was a tremendous sound. A major section of our glass bubble nose was blown out. Parts of the plane were flying through the sky. We knew we were in critical danger, but we headed east thinking that some way we'll make it out to the ocean."*

The plane was shaking and losing altitude. It took about five minutes to determine that it wasn't going to make it; the commander made the decision to bail out. The intercom radio had been blown out destroying communication between the six crew members in the front and the five gunners in the back. The radio man volunteered to take off his chute and crawl through the tunnel to the back of the plane. He found the tail gunner dead, but relayed the bail out message to the four remaining crewmembers.

At 18,000 ft., the outside air temperature gauge read thirty-one degrees below zero as Hap dropped out of the bomb bay. He had never made a parachute jump before and was never given any procedure to follow. He rolled over and over as he fell free. He wanted to get out of the bitter cold, so he let himself free fall until below 8000 ft., then pulled the cord, *"The chute opened all right but I was doing a wild violent swing in the chute."*

Still swinging wildly he descended to about 3000 ft., when three Japanese fighters appeared a couple miles away headed in his direction. They closed to within 600 ft. of Hap's chute and made a circle around it. Then two of them broke off and left while the other slowed and approached Hap. Japanese fighters were well known for their tactic of shooting holes into the chutes and watching as the fliers hurled to the ground. The fighter circled in a counter clockwise direction. He came within 100 ft. below and 200 ft. to the side of the chute. The fighter pulled abreast. Gripped with fear, Hap could see the pilot's face in the cockpit. To his astonishment, instead of firing at the chute, he saluted Hap, turned his fighter 180 degrees and flew off.

Hap hit the ground hard at high speed. The chute dragged him along the ground until he hit shrubbery and came to a stop. His back was severely injured, he couldn't get up; he lay there dazed.

"The civilians approached and began beating me with rocks, sticks and iron bars. They beat me to a pulp." Hap would no doubt have been killed had it not been for the arrival of a group of armed soldiers, who apparently had orders to capture B29 crew members for interrogation. Hap didn't know it at the time, but he was one of the lucky members of the crew. One gunner was killed by the fighters, three gunners never made it out of the plane, the engineer was killed in the jump and the bombardier was beaten to death by the civilians. Only five Rover Boys survived that day: the two pilots, the radio operator, the radar operator and Hap, the navigator.

They tied his hands behind his back, tied his feet together, put a rope around his neck and threw him in the back of a truck. He couldn't move, it was freezing cold, and he was uncontrollably urinating where he lay. When the truck made a stop, a lady ran up with a scissors and tried to get Hap's ring by attempting to cut his finger off. Luckily the truck moved on before the civilian had her way.

Hap estimates it took about two hours before they arrived at what turned out to be Kempei Tai torture prison in downtown Tokyo. He was kicked off the truck; still bound and tied he hit the ground hard. The soldiers took him into a building, approached a flight of stairs, and gave him a push. Not being able to protect himself, he toppled all the way to the bottom. The guards took him into a room, sat him at a table, interrogated him and beat him until he fainted.

When Hap regained consciousness, he found himself in a solitary caged cell. Twice a day the guards threw in a ball of rice that was infested with bugs, lice and fleas. He tried to eat, but his face was so beaten he couldn't get his mouth open. He consumed only water for a week until he could get his mouth open wide enough to force the rice in. No speaking was allowed; prisoners who spoke were killed. A flier in the cage next to Hap was hallucinating. He kept saying over and over, *"O.k. Mom, I'll be right down for breakfast, O.k. Mom I'll be right down for breakfast."* He was taken away and never seen again.

It was cold and much of the time was spent in total darkness. When he was able to produce a bowel movement, which wasn't very often, hogs on the outside of the wall would be waiting to consume it. *"I sat all day in the corner on the cold wooden floor with a thin shredded blanket; my clothes were torn, there were fleas, lice, open sores; I was all alone, my whole body was in pain and I couldn't talk to anybody. To me the loneliness and the silence hurt more than all the physical pain I endured. I cried a little; I cried a lot."*

Hap spent sixty-seven days in this solitary confinement including the night of March 10, 1945. It was after midnight, and the wind was blowing hard when Hap heard multi-engine planes overhead. At first he wondered where the Japanese got all those planes. Then the first bombs started to drop, the air raid sirens went off, and he knew the Americans were overhead. Hap's cell had a small opening that was normally covered by a dark cloth; however, that night the fierce winds created by the firestorm blew it off. Hap pulled himself off the floor and looked through the bars. All he could see was a solid red sky that was becoming brighter and brighter by the minute. The raid only lasted about two hours, but the fire grew in intensity after the bombing was over and it spread toward the prison. It burned through the night and into the morning. It finally burned itself out a half block from the prison entrance, the heat so great, that the wooden door to the cell compound burned off.

The B29 POW's lived in constant fear of execution

by beheading. Three weeks after the firestorm, the guards approached Hap's cell and announced that he was leaving. When the guards told him to take his shoes, he knew he wasn't coming back. Gripped with fear he slowly picked himself off the floor, gathered up his shoes and braced himself for his final day on earth. Hap followed the guards out of his cage.

Hap was pushed into the back of a truck, bound and blindfolded. The truck departed the prison with Hap as its sole cargo. It drove about three miles and stopped; the ties on Hap's feet were cut loose. He was ordered to climb a hill behind the truck, but he was so weak he kept falling down. When they reached the top he realized he was at a vacant zoo, where he was stripped naked, placed in an animal cage and ordered to hold onto the front bars. Civilians were paraded by to look at a B29 crewmember in hopes of convincing them that they had nothing to fear from an enemy this frail and weak. For Hap it was twenty four hours of pure humiliation.

When Hap was taken away from the zoo he was placed in a new facility, Tokyo's Omori prison. It wasn't exactly a Ritz Carelton, but for Hap it was close. Among the five-hundred prisoners, thirty-two B29 fliers were segregated, placed in the same enclosure and were allowed to talk to each other. *"We weren't out of danger. There were guards day and night with bayonets fixed, but to be with fellow Americans, to be able to talk, to see the sun and the stars at night, my whole world changed."* A couple of the guards showed compassion to the sick, starving emaciated fliers. One of the guards slipped Hap a piece of chocolate; an act of kindness he never forgot.

The Japanese surrendered after the atoms bombs were dropped on the cities of Hiroshima and Nagasaki. The prisoners were liberated August 29, 1945 and taken aboard the hospital ship, Benevolence, which was anchored in Tokyo bay. Hap weighed in at one hundred ten pounds, down from two hundred twelve, had his first shower in seven months and ate eighteen Milky Way bars in the first couple hours aboard. When he was strong enough to travel, he was flown to a hospital in Guam and later to another hospital in the States. He was discharged in 1946.

After the firestorm raid of March 10th, while Hap struggled to stay alive, Phil continued to fly combat missions over Japan. Ironically after surviving eight months and thirty-five missions, he was almost killed transporting a B29 home from Saipan after the war ended.

Following a fuel stop in Hawaii, Phil and his crew headed for San Francisco with a cargo of twenty marines. About half way across the Pacific Ocean, an engine failed and was shut down; shortly after, a second engine failed. The plane couldn't maintain altitude so Phil kept descending. He told the crew and the marines they may have to ditch, but for the thirty one men aboard there were only two seven man life rafts available. The B29 kept descending, until it was 50 ft. above the ocean. Phil was able to keep it flying at that altitude for the next two hundred miles until they reached San Francisco. They flew under the Golden Gate Bridge and on to Mather Air Base in Sacramento. The marines jumped out, kissed the ground and gave Phil a big hug. That was the last time Phil flew in a B29. He was discharged in October of 1945.

─────

The combat war in the Pacific was over, but the emotional war still raged in the minds and spirits of Phil and Hap. When Phil went back into civilian life he found it difficult to function. He had a girlfriend who had written him almost everyday when he was overseas. She eagerly traveled to San Francisco, for a reunion with Phil. It didn't take long for her to see that he was not in a state of mind that could maintain a relationship. *"I was no good; emotionally I was a wreck."* The reunion was short lived. She left for home, and although they talked in the future, they never saw each other again. The next few years were very tough. Phil joined his brother in business, but he couldn't concentrate and had difficulty fulfilling average day to day tasks. His brother had to do most of the work. Phil went to the Army for some help, only to hear that there were so many fliers suffering from Battle Fatigue, there weren't enough resources to help them. The Army's advice was to *"go home and try to get over it."*

Gradually Phil rebuilt his life, married and had children. He encouraged his teenage daughter to participate in a student exchange program with Japan. His daughter went to Japan to live with a family and learn about the Japanese culture. In turn, Phil's family housed two Japanese students eager to learn the American culture. Phil knew that sometime in the future, he would have to return to Japan.

By 1980 Phil was finally ready to make the pilgrimage back to Saipan and Japan. His travel partners were his wife and Johnnie's wife. Their first stop was Saipan. It had remnants of the past, but had changed along with the rest of the world. Phil visited his old airfield and stood on the spot, where he parked the Sentimental Journey after each mission. Johnnie's wife had never allowed herself to believe Johnnie was really dead. Phil helped her finally accept the reality that he was gone. In place of the military installation that Phil left behind, was a beautiful hotel resort, where Japanese newlyweds were on their honeymoons. What a difference forty years made!

The visit to Tokyo was also filled with mixed emotions. Except for a few open fields, the seventeen square miles destroyed by the firestorm had been rebuilt.

Phil tried to locate the center of the firestorm area and wondered, *"Is this where my bombs hit?"* He tried to act as any other tourist, but he had a paranoia that kept him thinking people were identifying him as the Pathfinder of March 10, 1945.

Like Phil, after he returned from the war, Hap couldn't sleep. At first he had vivid, frightening, nightmares almost every night. When he stayed in a hotel he had to tell the desk clerk not to be concerned, if someone heard screaming coming from his room. He tried hard to wipe out the memories that were tucked away in his head, but he was unsuccessful. After Hap was married, his wife and family did their best to help him work through many troubled nights. The nightmares became less frequent, but would never go away completely.

Hap had been thinking about going to Japan for many years. In 1984 he decided he needed some closure to the events that kept playing themselves over and over in his mind. He wrote to the U.S. government for help and approval. The U.S. ambassador to Japan assigned him an aide who set up the trip, tours, visits to places he wanted to see, and meetings with people to whom he wanted to speak. Hap embarked on what was would become the first of many trips back to Japan.

The Kempi Tai torture prison was located on the west side of Tokyo adjacent to the Sumida River. The headquarters and stables that housed the prisoners were gone, but the moat that Hap remembered was still there. He relived the partial memory of his night of terror, March 10, 1945. He walked across the bridges and looked to the east where Phil and the other three hundred and thirty four B29s had dropped their bombs. The young people on the streets could never imagine that today's gentle blue sky could have been such an angry red that night.

Hap returned to the village where he landed in his parachute. He was able to talk to many people who witnessed his capture and to some who were part of the mob that attacked him. Neither Hap nor the villagers held animosity toward one another. Each person recognized that the events of 1945 were ugly and left scars on everyone who had been caught up in them.

Hap returned nine times to Japan. He became a well known personality and was asked to speak at dozens of meetings and events. He eventually realized he had more friends in Japan than he had in the United States. He often visited them, and they often came to California to visit him. Of the hundreds of friends he made in Japan, two were special to him.

As the war was coming to an end and as Hap fought for survival in Omori prison, he was befriended by a prison guard. Kobyashi was a school master before the war and wasn't suited for the job he was assigned. A gentle and an inquisitive person, he was the guard who had slipped Hap the chocolate. Hap reunited with Kobyashi and returned his kindness by helping him come to the United States for schooling. Over the subsequent years, they were guests in each other's homes and became good friends.

Another and most important contact he was able to make was with a man named Hidechi. Hidechi was the fighter pilot who approached Hap when he was swinging in his chute, the pilot who chose to salute rather than shoot. He remembered that day as vividly as Hap. Hap asked him *"Why did you allow me to live instead of shooting me?"*

He answered, *"Some of us as fliers, had integrity and dignity. Some of us had honor and respect for fellow fliers."*

On one of his last visits to Japan, Hidechi's son contacted Hap, informed him that his father had died and requested that Hap attend the funeral. The feelings of gratitude welled up in Hap as he looked for the last time at the man who spared his life. Hap brought his hand to his forehead, saluted the honorable flier and bowed his head as he left the sanctuary.

In 2009 Phil turned eighty-eight and Hap turned eighty-seven. They both became very successful businessmen and neither retired before he reached eighty. Age has attacked their short term memories, but not their recollections of 1944 and 1945. They remember names, dates, times and events as if they happened yesterday. Phil and Hap know they were the lucky ones and because of that they will carry guilt until they die.

Hap summed it up the best, *"TIME HEALS EVERY-THING…..almost."*

Quonset hut on Saipan

B 29's lining up for the 1500 mile flight to Tokyo

View from nose of B-29 Bomber passing Mt. Fuji enroute to Tokyo target.

Bombs away over Tokyo

Great Day! Liberation from Tokyo POW Camp on August 29, 1945
Hap (circled)

Rover Boys Express.
Hap (top center) and only four others survived Jan. 27th 1945

Tales from the Sky Kitchen Cafe

THE XPERT

Tales from the Sky Kitchen Cafe

THE XPERT

By 1978 when I joined the fraternity at the center counter of the Sky Kitchen, there were already many senior members. Syl was a guy about fifteen years older than I, and he was the resident expert on anything and everything. Because he was so well known for his talent, he provided himself with a personalized license plate which simply read XPERT.

Normally, this would have been a sign of arrogance, but with Syl it seemed to fit. When you asked him a question, the answer was usually correct; when it wasn't, he delivered the answer in a manner that made you believe it was.

Syl was into gadgets. He flew a nice four seat airplane that had all the up-to-date gadgets. He had the first moving map I'd ever seen. Nowadays, almost every new car has a GPS with a moving map and many telephones also have them. In the early 1980's no one had seen such a thing; Syl's map was out on the cutting edge. Right in line with his love for gadgets, Syl discovered the personal computer way ahead of the rest of us. Before I was aware of personal computers, Syl was already an expert on them. He went through computers almost as fast as I went through a dozen eggs. It seemed he always had a new computer and often two.

Syl had one mandatory requirement for every computer he

bought. It had to be a Mac. He hated PC's, he hated Windows operating systems, and he hated Microsoft. We had no idea why he was so opinionated, but we accepted it. After all he was the expert. Syl went so far as to set up a web site which showed an animated character holding a Mac and peeing on a PC. Luckily, Bill Gates never knew what trouble he was in!

After the laptop computer became as popular as the cell phone, Syl changed the environment around the center counter; he started bringing his computer to lunch with him. All of a sudden it began to look like Starbucks. Many of the other regulars began bringing their laptops to the Sky Kitchen so that they could keep up with Syl, but he was still the guru, still the expert.

Syl had an exterior facade that made him appear ornery and cantankerous. Often he would seem irritated by a mundane question that was asked him, but most of us knew it was only a thin veil. Syl loved the questions and loved giving his answers. Down deep he was a softy and wouldn't hesitate to throw a dollar on the counter for my coffee, after helping me with my learning process.

In the 1990's, Syl started to develop medical problems and it was harder and harder for him to keep his medical certificate which he needed to fly airplanes. He had to stop flying, but he still continued coming to the Sky Kitchen every day for lunch.

In 1998 I sat next to Syl at lunch one day and told him my wife and I were moving two hundred miles north to be with the kids and grandkids. He looked at me and said, *"Why would you leave the best place on earth with the best pilot rendezvous in the world, to live in a little town up north?"* Luckily for the expert, his grandkids lived in the San Francisco Bay Area.

I fly down to the Sky Kitchen on a regular basis and have the best of both worlds. Syl is now in his mid-eighties but is still there every day with his laptop open. He's as ornery as ever, but he'll still buy my coffee even though it's up to three dollars. Syl has had several bouts with cancer. He's gotten thinner and it looks as if his height has shrunk an inch or two. He's given up on belts, and he keeps his pants up with suspenders. I notice he has a cane that I'm sure was forced on him by an expert from the medical profession.

After a recent lunch at the Sky Kitchen I walked with Syl to the parking lot. There sat the most gorgeous red Ferrari sports car I'd ever seen. He opened the door, exposing the soft, tan, leather seats, and threw his cane onto the back seat. He yanked the blue handicap placard off his mirror and somehow slipped into the driver seat. As the engine roared and Syl drove off, I immediately noticed that he had given up the XPERT license plate. The new one read OXSIMRN.

The Xpert leaping into his new car

The Xpert's new license plate

JUST A PRIVATE PILOT

Tales from the Sky Kitchen Cafe

JUST A PRIVATE PILOT

While most of us at the center counter earned our private pilot licenses without really knowing how we would use them, Reid had a clear vision for his and wasted no time making it a reality. Reid wanted to get a multi-engine rating, buy a twin engine airplane, and use it for business as well as long distance adventure. By 1963 before he had logged ninety-five hours of flight time, he had earned his multi-engine rating, and had bought a used six seat twin.

Reid was successful in the financial field and had worked his way up to become president of the Commonwealth Group of mutual funds. He immediately put his plane to work. Commonwealth had a distributor of their funds in St. Louis, Missouri. Before fax machines, computers and cell phones, personal contact was the best way to disseminate information. Reid would fly his twin from California to Missouri, pick up the sales manager, hop all over the Midwest, and land at lonely airports to meet with salesmen who worked out of tiny one-man offices. After breakfast in one town, lunch in another, and dinner in yet another, Reid would give a little talk about his mutual funds and why they were doing so well. The salesmen would leave the meetings, contact the farmers and merchants and say, *"I just had breakfast with the president of this mutual fund and he told me etc. etc."* A week after one of those trips, Reid would watch the sales graphs shoot straight up. The little airplane was paying for itself.

By 1970 Reid had sold his used twin and had bought a new one. It was the same make and model, a Cessna 320 Skyknight, but in this one, he installed all the up to date equipment. Reid was now the president of the American Express International Fund which had many investors in Europe and the Middle East. He quickly realized that this presented an opportunity for adventure. At dinner one night, he said to his wife, *"Hey Peggy, how would you like to fly to Europe in our Skyknight?"*

Flying to Europe in a small plane is quite different from flying there in a jet airliner. Navigation, communication, weather, winds, and re-fueling stops have to be given careful consideration. Reid's friend John, also a pilot, was enlisted to help plan and be the co-pilot for the trip. On the morning of April 30th, 1970, after six months of planning, Reid, Peggy, and John, fired up the engines of the Skyknight and departed on their journey, leaving San Carlos, California and the Sky Kitchen behind them.

The plane normally has six seats. For this trip, the back two seats were removed to make room for containers, which held twenty-six gallons of additional fuel. The extra tanks were plumbed into the existing fuel system and could be accessed through valves placed in the cockpit. This provided the travelers with an extra hour of endurance in the air which would be used if strong headwinds were encountered or if they had to turn around and return to a previous landing site. The standard radios in the plane were operated on the VHF (very high frequency) band and limited the long-range communication ability of the Skyknight. Reid purchased a large HF (high frequency) radio. He placed it in front of one of the center seats which by then had been piled high with aviation charts. The HF radio could be accessed by either pilot, and it extended their range of communication. Peggy sat in the other center seat, Reid and John occupied the two front seats.

Cruising at 180 knots (207 MPH) with stops along the way, it took three days to cross the United States and reach Montreal, Canada. The most easterly province of Canada is Newfoundland-Labrador. Reid had decided that Goose Bay, Labrador would be their launching point over the North Atlantic.

The trio departed Goose Bay on May 2nd and set a course for Greenland. Four hours later the Skyknight was being refueled at Narsarssauq. The next day after checking the forecasts for weather and winds, Reid lifted the twin off the runway and headed east. Another four hours later, they landed at Reykjavik, Iceland.

The travelers loved Iceland. As a bonus for their flight, a volcano erupted the day after they arrived, and they were able to fly over it and get fantastic photos. Three days were spent on the island before departing on the final leg across the Atlantic Ocean. From Iceland Reid took a south easterly course which would bring them in another four hours to Stornaway, an island in the Outer Hebrides off the west coast of Scotland.

The total flying time from Canada to Scotland had been only twelve hours, but it had taken constant vigilance to monitor the course, the weather, and the airplane.

Today pilots have the luxury of GPS (Global Positioning System), a system that can take an airplane to within a few feet of a destination. In 1970 the only navigation device that could be used in the North Atlantic was an NDB (Non Directional Beacon). The pilot would tune in the station and follow an instrument needle which pointed toward the beacon. The problem with the system was the apparatus didn't know from where the wind was coming. A strong crosswind could blow a plane in a circle around a beacon, while the needle still pointed straight at it.

Reid flew between 10,000 and 12,000 feet where he could talk to airliners overhead, getting reports for the weather ahead. He was in contact with air traffic controllers to whom he would give reports of his approximate position. He also monitored the emergency frequency, where local controllers could locate the Skyknight on their radar and give it a corrected heading, if unexpected winds had blown it off its course.

Each of the planes two engines had its own set of gauges which had to be constantly monitored. If one engine were to develop a serious problem, it could be shut down and the plane could continue to fly at a lower altitude, on the remaining engine. There were also several gauges for the fuel. There were two fuel gauges for the main tanks which were mounted on the tips of the wings, but no gauges for the auxiliary tanks or for the reservoir tank in the back of the cabin. The pilots had to pay close attention to what fuel had been used and where their remaining fuel was stored. The trip had been planned for four hour legs between landings, but the plane had six and a half hours of fuel on board. The extra hours of fuel had given Reid a cushion to deal with head winds or mechanical problems.

Europe was a pilot's paradise. Distances were short and flying from one country to another was relatively easy. The trio flew from Stornaway to Edinburgh and a few days later to London. From England it was on to Germany, stopping in Hamburg, Frankfurt, Stuttgart, and Munich; then they headed to Italy, Brussels, Amsterdam and Zurich, ending back in London on June 5th.

Peggy and John bought tickets on the airlines and Reid's oldest son, John Jr. joined him for the trip back home. The trip was uneventful, but Reid needed a respite from long distance flying.

It wasn't until two years later in 1972, that he decided to make the trip again. This time he used the plane to visit investors, banks and businesses which were associated with the mutual funds he represented. The flight over was a repeat of the previous flight of 1970. Once he got there, however, he had some unusual experiences.

As a consequence of Germany's defeat in World War II and the onset of the Cold War, the country was split into two states: West Germany and East Germany. In both states former occupying troops, Russian in the east and American in the west, were permanently stationed. The former German capital, Berlin, was a special case; it was divided into East Berlin and West Berlin, with West Berlin completely surrounded by East German territory.

Automobiles and trains were allowed to travel through East Germany to reach West Berlin, but there were designated transit routes. All travelers needed transit visas and check points were established. Three corridors were established for air travel mainly to accommodate commercial and military aircraft. Reid had a meeting scheduled with the banking commissioner in West Berlin, and he thought it would be fun to fly the southern corridor from Frankfurt into West Berlin.

Only American, British or French registered aircraft were allowed to fly the corridors. Since his plane was U.S. registered, he applied to the State Department for permission. After a lengthy application process, Reid was granted permission, but was required to go to the airbase in Frankfurt to receive a briefing on how to fly the corridor.

Reid was directed to a Lieutenant Colonel. *"You want to do what?"*

"Fly the corridor into Berlin," Reid replied.

The officer looked incredulously at the paperwork, shrugged and said, *"Well I guess I'll have to give you a briefing."* They went upstairs to a briefing room and the Colonel began. *"Number one, if a Russian Mig flies alongside you and waggles his wings and you know you're in the corridor, ignore him. Number two, if he comes alongside you and waggles his wings and you know you're outside the corridor, you better follow him. Number three, if you don't know whether you're inside or outside the corridor, I think you better follow him also."*

That got Reid's attention. *"What happens when I follow him?"*

"He'll take you to an East German airfield. You'll ask to speak to a Russian officer, because we don't recognize the East German government."

While Reid was digesting this information the Colonel continued, *"You'll get one phone call."*

"Who would you suggest I call?" Reid asked.

The officer smiled and said, *"If I were you I'd call the idiots in Bonn who gave you permission to do this in the first place."*

The trip provided none of the excitement predicted by the Colonel. Reid landed at Berlin's Templehof airport without incident, taxied to the fuel station, and learned that his was the first aircraft to purchase aviation gas in the last five months. Needless to say it wasn't difficult to find a place to park.

Reid decided, since he had his plane in Europe, he might as well fly to Asia and visit some clients in the Middle East. American Express had set up a mutual fund designed for investors in the Middle East. They had formed a marketing partnership with the Kuwait Investment Company.

Reid and a business companion first flew the Skyknight to Beirut, Lebanon. Unlike its condition today, Beirut was the most beautiful city in the region. It was described for decades as the Paris of the Middle East. From Beirut, Reid had planned to fly directly to Kuwait, but he was not able to get the clearance, and instead found himself on the way to Damascus, Syria. He landed in Damascus with much trepidation. The United States did not have diplomatic relations with Syria, so it was no surprise to see machine guns aimed at his U.S. registered plane as he taxied to the terminal.

In order to fly the shortest route from Damascus to Kuwait, it was necessary to fly along the border of Iraq. Reid needed advice regarding what navigation to use in order to avoid Iraqi airspace. He found a fellow who appeared to have the information he needed. The fellow said *"Do you have an ax on board?"*

Astonished, Reid said, *"I'm flying across the desert, why would I need an ax?"*

"Well there's a navigation beacon, but it hasn't worked for six months. The most reliable navigation is to follow the Trans Arabian Pipeline that runs just south of the Iraqi border all the way to Kuwait."

Reid nodded his head and asked *"How about the ax? What do we need an ax for?"*

The man suddenly realized he had left out the most important piece of information. *"Oh yes, there's a service road that runs right next to the pipeline. If you get into trouble, you can land on the road. Take your ax and chop a hole in the pipeline. When you get a big enough puddle of oil on the ground, someone will come out to see what's wrong, and they'll find you. Otherwise you might be stuck in the desert forever."*

Luckily, the ax stayed in its sheath all the way to Kuwait.

———

However…Reid's greatest adventure was yet to come!

———

As the century entered its last decade, two aircraft restoration projects, totally independent of each other, were under way. By 1997 they would meld together as part of a grand flying odyssey.

The first project was designed and funded by Reid. He had purchased a military surplus amphibian, an aircraft which lands on either land or water. It was a 1955 Grumman Albatross. The Albatross was designed to be a patrol aircraft for the Navy. Of the four hundred sixty-five built, about thirty are privately owned and are flying today. The Albatross has its wings on the top of the fuselage with one engine mounted to each wing. The landing gear (wheels) is retractable and deployed, when landing on a runway, but left retracted, when landing on water. As a private plane it would be considered quite large. Looking at it from the terminal, one might mistake it for a commercial commuter plane.

Reid poured his heart, soul and checkbook into the restoration. He re-designed the wings and rebuilt the engines. He designed his own instrument panel and added state of the art avionics, including two GPS (global positioning system) units. Mechanically, it was perfect, but he wasn't done. The outside was re-painted in a beautiful light blue and gray color scheme, very similar to the one used on Air Force One, the U.S. President's plane. The interior resembles a fine sailing yacht, blending teakwood and leather. It has a galley, dining booth, lavatory and six first class passenger seats. Hours and hours were spent negotiating with the Federal Aviation Administration for certification, and by 1996 the Albatross was authorized to fly.

In San Antonio, Texas, the second restoration project was being undertaken by a female pilot, Linda Finch. Her vision was to acquire a Lockheed Electra 10E, the same plane flown by Amelia Earhart in 1937 on her ill fated attempt to circle the globe. Once the plane was restored, she planned to re-create Amelia's route and circumnavigate the earth at or near the equator. Her goal was to pay tribute to the lost aviator, departing sixty years to the day after Earhart did.

Pratt & Whitney, the original manufacturer of the Electra's engines, became the primary sponsor. In the 1930's, only fifteen Electra 10E's were manufactured. By 1993, only two were known to exist. Linda was able to acquire one of them and it arrived by trailer at her San Antonio Hangar. It was a mess. It hadn't flown in decades; the wings and engines weren't attached and it had corrosion attacking many of its parts. The restoration team studied old photos and blueprints in order to repair and restore corroded parts. Two rebuilt Pratt & Whitney engines were attached. The plane was fitted with much more sophisticated navigation and radio equipment than Amelia's, but otherwise it was exactly the same plane. Miraculously in three years the replica of Amelia Earhart's silver metal 1935 Electra 10E was ready to fly.

As Reid's Albatross was nearing completion, his crew chief, Andy, who had done some work for Linda, heard that she was looking for a companion plane to fly along with her to take photos and videos of her flight. Reid's plane was perfect for the mission. It was large and could carry several photographers along with their equipment, and possessed an added bonus. If the Electra had problems and had to ditch in the ocean, the Albatross could land on the water and pick up Linda and her co-pilot. Linda was contacted, and immediately agreed to include Reid, and his Albatross. Both crews began preparing for the trip, which was publicized as World Flight 1997.

On March 17, 1937, Amelia Earhart lifted her Electra off the runway at Oakland, California. On March 17, 1997, Linda lifted her Electra off the same runway with Reid's Albatross right behind her. The Electra housed Linda and her navigator. The Albatross carried Reid, his co-pilot, his crew chief, his wife Peggy, two still photographers, a video photographer, and a newspaper reporter.

The airplanes made their way across the United States, and

left it behind as they departed Miami. After a stop in Puerto Rico, they headed south to reach South America, where a stop was made in Venezuela. The next day brought them to one of the most interesting stops on the trip, Paramaribo, Suriname. It boasted one of the longest runways in South America. It had been lengthened during World War II to handle the heavily loaded airplanes which hauled bauxite back to the United States, where it was used to produce aluminum.

Suriname, originally named Dutch Guiana, is a small, little known former Dutch colony tucked in the northeast corner of the continent. The total population is around four hundred fifty thousand. Reid had never seen a country made up of such a diversity of ethnic cultures. A large influx of traders, slaves, settlers, laborers, and others from all areas of the world including Holland, Britain, India, Indonesia, Israel, China, West Africa, and elsewhere have made the population one of the most diverse on the continent. Yet the country is free of racial discrimination and tension. Reid, Linda and the entire entourage was invited to the American Ambassador's residence where musicians representing the different ethnic groups performed together in a percussion group, each with his original ethnic instruments. The sound was one that could not be duplicated anywhere else in the world. Reid and his wife Peggy promised each other to return one day to Paramaribo.

The Electra led the way to Brazil, where the city of Natal sits on the most easterly tip of South America. This was to be the launching point to cross the South Atlantic to Dakar, Senegal on the west coast of Africa. The flight plan called for a twelve hour, sixteen hundred-fifty nautical mile flight over the water. In order to carry enough fuel, only Reid, his co-pilot and the crew chief would make the flight. The other passengers had to travel to Sao Paulo, take an Air France flight to Paris and another from

Paris to Dakar, where they met up with the Albatross. Take off took place at four-thirty in the afternoon. The Albatross was leveled off at just twelve hundred ft. above the ocean as they flew off into the darkness. The coast of Africa showed up at dawn. Reid landed in daylight at Dakar just a few minutes after Linda had touched down.

Heading east, the planes landed at exotic places including Malaga, Spain, Tunis, Tunisia, Athens, Greece, Luxor, Egypt, Karachi, Pakistan, and Calcutta, India. Up to this point the team had not encountered a drop of rain. Southeast Asia is known for its monsoonal rains, as Amelia Earhart found out in 1937. She was deluged by rain, which fell so savagely it beat the paint from the leading edges of her wings and kept her grounded for days. As Linda and Reid flew through Thailand and Singapore, they started to encounter the signs of an approaching monsoon. They put their planes down in Surabaya, Indonesia, and, just as they had for Amelia, the relentless rains arrived with vengeance.

Two days later, when the storm had passed, the Electra and the Albatross departed and followed Amelia's route over the lush green lands of Indonesia. The next stop was Darwin, Australia, where the planes were thoroughly checked for the long flights ahead over the Pacific Ocean. The odyssey continued over New Guinea as the team made its way toward Howland Island.

In 1937 Amelia Earhart left New Guinea and headed east over the Pacific Ocean. Her navigator, Fred Noonan, known to be the best over-water navigator of that era, was plotting a course to find the tiny piece of land known as Howland Island, which lay twenty five hundred miles ahead. It was there that Amelia would refuel for the next leg to Honolulu.

Earhart and Noonan had flown through the night for twenty-two hours. They were confined in a plane that reeked from gasoline fumes, and they were exhausted and running low on fuel. In addition, because of low clouds, they were down to 1000 ft. off the water and looking into the sun for a speck of land that measured less than a half-mile wide and one and a half miles long. A navy ship, the Itasca, was purposely positioned near Howland to help guide Amelia to the island. She made contact with the ship, when she was within two hundred miles of the island, but the reception was weak and little communication took place. Further complicating her plight, Amelia had chosen to leave behind a piece of radio equipment which would have allowed the ship to pinpoint her position. Experts feel that the Electra may have been within thirty miles of Howland Island, when it ran out of fuel and was lost forever in the sea.

World Flight 1997 had no problem finding Howland Island. Technology had given them the use of GPS navigation and on board flight computers. In 1937 it was almost impossible to find the island; in 1997 it was almost impossible to miss it. Before leaving Howland Island, the planes circled it and dropped a wreath in memory of Amelia Earhart and Fred Noonan. A stop was made in Hawaii, before the team headed for home. After one hundred ninety-five hours of flying and covering a distance of 26,347 nautical miles, Linda's Electra and Reid's Albatross landed in Oakland, California on the same runway from which they had departed two and a half months earlier.

Since 1964, Reid has amassed about nine thousand hours of flying time. He's flown to six continents, dozens of countries, and piloted over two million miles. He's added numerous ratings to his original pilot license along the way, but he has never obtained a commercial or air transport license. He loves to say, *"I flew all those adventures as just a private pilot."*

First Albatross to Circumnavigate the World   March 17 to May 29, 1997

26,347 Nautical Miles

Oakland, CA Burbank, CA Tucson, AZ New Orleans, LA
Miami, FL San Juan, PR Cumana, Venezuela Paramaribo,
Suriname Fortaleza, Brazil Natal, Brazil Dakar, Senegal Las
Palmas, Canary Islands Malaga, Spain Tunis, Tunisia Athens,
Greece Luxor, Egypt Dubai, UAE Karachi, Pakistan Calcutta,
India Chiang Mai, Thailand Bankok, Thailand Singapore
Jakarta, Indonesia Surabaya Darwin, AUS Port Moresby, Papua
New Guinea Nadzab, Papua New Guinea Nauru, Oceania
Tarawa, KIR Howland Island Kanton Island Christmas Island
Honolulu, HI Oakland, CA

Reid's route around the world

The Albatross over the San Francisco Golden Gate Bridge

The Albatross at 500 ft. above the ground

Reid back at Oakland airport after 26,347 miles

Tales from the Sky Kitchen Cafe

FEAR OF FLYING

Tales from the Sky Kitchen Cafe

FEAR OF FLYING

Women have a rich aviation history. In 1911 the first woman was licensed to fly in the United States. In 1918 the first woman was hired as an airmail pilot, and in 1929 the first woman was hired as a stunt pilot for motion pictures. Amelia Earhart made history in the 1930's; and during World War II, a corps of women, the Wasps (Women Air force Service Pilots) flew non-combat missions for the Army Air Corps.

In spite of women's contributions to aviation men have dominated the flying community, since the Wright brothers first flew a powered plane in 1903. It was 1973 before the first woman was hired in the United States as a pilot on a major airline. In 2007 there were 115,000 commercial pilots in the country, but only 7,100 were female.

Despite their minority women were no strangers to the center counter at the Sky Kitchen. On any given day there would be at least two or three women pilots eating burgers and trading stories with the guys. Jeanne was one of them.

Jeanne graduated high school in 1946 and decided she wanted to learn to fly. Her dad said, *"If you can pay for it, you can do it."* Jeanne saved every penny she could from part-time jobs and came up with the eleven dollars per hour to pay for the plane and the instructor. (Today a student pays one hundred fifty dollars per hour). She not only earned a private pilot license but over the years added a commercial license and a flight instructor license.

Jeanne was always searching for a way to give back to aviation for all the joy and adventures it had given her. An opportunity arose in 1978 when Jeanne's friend Fran came to her with a problem. Fran's husband had been a radar specialist in the Navy before his recent retirement. While testing radar equipment, he survived two plane accidents and vowed never to get into an airplane again. A trip was being planned to Australia and Fran said to Jeanne, *"I don't mind taking a ship to get there, but I'll be damned, if I'll take it back home. We have to get this guy in the air!"*

Jeanne and Fran belonged to an organization of women pilots. After talking to friends in the group, they found there were programs in other parts of the country that helped people like Fran's husband, conquer their fear of airplanes. The two women researched the techniques and were successful with Fran's husband. Although he was afraid of turbulence, he slept through the bumpy flight all the way to Australia. From this experience, they co-founded the Fear of Flying Clinic in Northern California.

In order to help more than one person at a time, Jeanne and her friend believed they would need to create a seminar atmosphere and enlist the help of professionals. Jeanne acted as a moderator and a behavioral counselor volunteered her time. Realizing that professionals have more credibility than lay persons, they enlisted help from airline pilots, flight attendants, maintenance personnel and air traffic controllers. Along with other volunteers their faculty was complete. Their credo was "knowledge dispels fear."

The clinics were set up to begin every three months. They were limited to twenty-five students, all of whom committed their time for two consecutive weekends. On the very first day of the clinic, all twenty-five were immediately exposed to the flying environment.

Weekend 1–Day 1:

Many people are afraid to even set foot in an airport. In order to help desensitize them, the group meets in the Reflection Room at the International Terminal of the San Francisco Airport. The room overlooks the gates which house the large aircraft that fly overseas. They witness up close the size of the planes and the hundreds of people scurrying through the airport.

The behavioral counselor gathers the group in a circle and begins a go around. The first step to dispelling fear is to identify why one is afraid. Some people are able to verbalize their fears, others need help to identify them. Once the fears are identified, Jeanne, the moderator, can address them.

The common fears start to surface.

"I flew once. The plane got into turbulence and started to shake. I was scared to death, I was sure it would break apart."

"How many of you are scared by the turbulence?" Jeanne asks. Every hand goes up.

"The airplane doesn't even care about turbulence. It's engineered and built to withstand much more than bumpy air. Turbulence doesn't cause planes to break apart. The plane just keeps flying whether the air is smooth or rough." Most of the students are skeptical, but over the next four days they will hear the explanation over and over again.

An older woman in the second row raises her hand. *"Why are there so many noises inside the airplane? They're spooky."*

"That's a great question. Think about it. Airplanes are complex

machines. The noises should be thought of as positive instead of negative. The huge engines make noise as they operate; the flaps make noise as they extend to slow the plane and the landing gear makes noise as it places the wheels in position for landing. What would be spooky is if the noises weren't there."

A muscular young guy who looked like nothing could scare him chimed in. "I'm afraid of heights. I can't even look over a balcony from the fifth floor of a building."

Jeanne had heard this many times before. "It's interesting; the view from an airplane is quite different than from a balcony. In the plane we're enclosed. There is no feeling of falling off an edge. It's actually a beautiful view."

The fears keep surfacing. "I'm claustrophobic; the thought of being squeezed into a little space is terrifying."

"Have you ever seen the inside of an airliner?" Jeanne responded.

"No."

"It's not what you think. You're not in capsule; you're in a large room. People get out of their seats, walk around, and even go to the restroom. The inside of the airliner is a lot bigger than the room we're in right now. Do you feel claustrophobic in here?"

"Not really."

After an hour of questions, Jeanne introduces a former graduate, who tells his story. To the students it's the same as their story. The difference is the graduate has conquered his fear and the students have not. Yet, as they leave for the day, the students are starting to believe.

Weekend 1–Day 2:

Today Jeanne introduces an airline pilot who is dressed in his uniform. He explains the education it takes to fly an airplane and the mandatory recurrent training, that is required to maintain those skills.

"It took me ten years to become an airline pilot. I started in little planes and worked my way up. Each step of the way I had to take examinations and check rides with examiners. Now that I fly for an airline, every six months I have to go into a simulator and prove that I still have the skills to do my job."

The captain paused, and then continued. *"And by the way all of us have to pass a medical exam every six months. If we don't pass we don't fly."*

The pilot is followed to the podium by a uniformed flight attendant. After a brief explanation of her duties, a student asks, *"Why is that bell always chiming in the cabin of the plane?"*

The flight attendant laughs, *"It may sound like something important, but it's usually the pilot asking us to bring him his coffee."*

After lunch everybody heads to the maintenance terminal for a tour. The comments start coming from the group.

"It's amazing. Look how meticulous they are."

"I never realized how much time is spent making planes ready. Never!"

Weekend 2–Day 1:

The day starts with a tour of the Control Tower at the San Francisco International Airport. The tower has a spectacular 360-degree view of the entire airport. There are four controllers working in the tower, each one with binoculars around his neck. The chief of the tower addresses the group.

"Each crew has four controllers and we rotate them so that we have 24/7 coverage."

A student raises his hand. *"How do you keep all these planes from bumping into each other?"*

"We know where every airplane is whether it's on the ground or in the air. Any plane that wants to taxi must get permission from the controller who watches the ground. He uses his binoculars to identify the plane

and makes sure it's clear for the plane to move from one spot on the field to another."

"How do you see them in the air?" The student asks.

The chief points to a monitor with a green lighted screen. *"This is one of our radar screens. Every plane has a device that is transmitting its position onto this screen. We keep all the planes at a safe distance from each other."*

As everyone crowds around the screen, the chief continues. *"When an airplane leaves the airspace that we control, it is passed on to another controller in a different facility who puts it on his radar screen. The plane is constantly monitored until it lands at its destination and taxis to the terminal."*

In the afternoon the second tour of the day takes place. Everyone boards a vacant airplane for an imaginary flight. They sit in the seats, walk around, listen to the bells going on and off, and even use the restrooms. The students are ready!

Weekend 2–Day 2:

Graduation day! The final exam is an actual flight on a jet airliner. All of the class members have reserved seats on a regularly scheduled roundtrip flight between San Francisco and Los Angeles; each direction has a flight time of an hour.

In each row of three seats there are two members of the class with a volunteer graduate from a previous class in between them. Standing near the still open door of the plane, Jeanne raises her hand for silence. *"The doors will be closing shortly and we will be taking off for L.A. I have confidence that everyone on the plane is ready for the flight, but if anyone feels he can't confront it, you now have the option to leave the plane. Once we start to taxi, it will be too late."*

A long silence follows her words but no one stirs from his seat. In the thirty-two years of this program, only three people have taken up Jeanne's offer.

The doors are closed and the Captain's voice booms through the cabin. *"Congratulations to all of you and welcome aboard. The weather looks good and we should have a smooth flight. If you need anything, please ask your flight attendant. We'll be in Los Angeles in fifty-eight minutes."*

A lunch is arranged in Los Angeles as the group waits for the return flight. Every student is given a graduation certificate and each shares a comment with the class.

A woman in her forties stands up. *"I can't believe it. I applied for my first passport yesterday."*

The muscular young man speaks. *"Thanks Jeanne, you helped me buy a ticket to the world."*

The final speaker, a woman in her sixties, stands with tears in her eyes. *"My grandkids live in New Zealand. I've never seen them. I'm finally going to meet my grandchildren. Finally!"*

Fear is a primal emotion, and we need fear to warn us against danger. Often, however, unfounded fears can freeze us and keep us from accomplishing tasks that we want or need to perform; they can also limit our enjoyment of life. Jeanne has helped over two thousand people conquer their fear of flying, and has truly given back to aviation.

In 1936 Beryl Markham, a pioneer Aviatrix, flew the first east to west transatlantic flight from Europe to North America in a single engine plane. She admitted she had to conquer fear as her plane left the coast of England. She wrote: *"The fear is gone now—not overcome nor reasoned away. It is gone because something else has taken its place; the confidence and trust, the inherent belief in the security of land underfoot—now this faith is transferred to my plane, because the land has vanished and there is no other tangible thing to fix faith upon. Flight is but momentary escape from the eternal custody of earth."*

Tales from the Sky Kitchen Cafe

UPSIDE DOWN

Tales from the Sky Kitchen Cafe

Upside Down

Norm started flying in 1964 and enjoyed taking his family and friends on trips around the country and to Baja, Mexico. After twenty years, Norm was confident he could get from point A to point B with no trouble and he felt his challenges as a pilot were slowly disappearing. He said to his wife, *"I'm getting bored just flying an airplane in an upright position all the time."* While most pilots spend their flying careers working hard to accomplish just that, Norm wanted to experience inverted flight.

Aerobatics could be described as acrobatics performed in an airplane, while rarely in an upright position. Norm had previously taken a few aerobatic lessons. He loved the thrill of the maneuvers and the confidence it gave him to feel completely in control. He decided his future flying experiences would no longer be always in straight, level, and upright positions; as often as possible, they would be upside down.

Norm had graduated college with a degree in aeronautical engineering, but had gone into sales and had never put his engineering education to use. Now he found a use for his engineering background; he was going to build an aerobatic airplane.

The concept of homebuilt airplanes was not a new

one. There are dozens of companies who provide manufactured pieces for their planes and deliver them in kit form. As one section is assembled, a kit arrives with the pieces for the next section, until eventually the entire craft is put together. The builder then has to paint it, install his own engine, propeller, instruments, and radio gear. The FAA (Federal Aviation Administration) has inspectors who are required to give their sign-off during certain phases of construction. When the plane is finally finished, a regulation requires twenty hours of limited flight, before it is given a license in a category termed Experimental. Homebuilts have an excellent safety record and there are thousands flying today.

One such company was started by Frank Christensen, a self made millionaire, who later entered the aviation industry by designing oil systems for aerobatic airplanes. His vision was to develop a home built aerobatic aircraft, which could be constructed with relative ease by anyone, regardless of a background in aircraft construction or engineering. He also wanted it to be a craft that could be used for competition, advanced aerobatic training, and sport cross country flying. Christensen formed a company in 1977 and his Christen Eagle II made its debut at the famous Oshkosh Fly-in, the largest aeronautical show in North America. The Eagle was immediately popular with both amateur and professional aerobatic pilots. Since 1977, more than a thousand Eagle II's have been built.

In 1985 Norm received a shipment containing Kit #1 for his Christen Eagle. He set up a shop in his garage, where he could spend time on the project after work and on the weekends. It was a slow and arduous process. After eight years and twenty-five hundred hours spent in his garage, the project was moved to a hangar at San Carlos airport, where the beautiful two seat biplane was completed. Its first test flight took place in 1993.

Norm found an aerobatic instructor, who was willing to take him on as a student. The instructor was also an aerobatic competitor. He told Norm, *"If I'm going to teach you aerobatics, I'm going to teach you to competition standards."* Norm had no inclination to become a competitor, but was pleased to find an instructor with standards that matched his own.

Training began with the four basic maneuvers which are the foundation of aerobatic flying: rolls, loops, spins and hammerheads.

A roll resembles a screw that is being turned. The pilot slowly turns the plane upside down and then continues the turn until it is right side up. The screw can be turned while flying horizontally, vertically or anywhere in between.

A loop could be described as flying a plane around the outside of an imaginary Ferris wheel. It starts at the bottom of the wheel and continues over the top until it returns to where it began.

A spin takes place when the pilot pushes the nose of the plane above the horizon and lets the speed get so slow that the plane stops flying. It noses over and turns in a spiral motion as it heads toward the ground.

With a hammerhead maneuver the pilot uses his speed and power to turn the craft straight up into the sky. When the plane runs out of speed, it stops in mid air with the nose facing straight up. It flips over and accelerates as it heads toward the earth.

Once the aerobatic pilot has command of the four basic maneuvers, he can then combine them in all sorts of different sequences. He can roll the plane while going straight up until it hammerheads, and then he can spin it as it heads toward earth. He can loop the plane while rolling it around the Ferris wheel and then spin it on the way down. There are endless numbers of sequences the pilot can make up and execute.

After about a year of practicing the maneuvers, Norm still didn't think he was interested in competition, but he decided to enter a contest just to see, if he had the skills needed for it. He entered a contest called, The Los Angeles Gold Cup. It was hosted in Taft, California, located in the southwestern corner of the San Joaquin Valley, or, as Norm described it, *"in the boonies."*

He entered at the lowest level, the Sportsman category, and to his surprise he won. He didn't know it then, but that contest was the beginning of a journey, one that would consume him with a passion that still drives him today.

The competitions have levels of progression based on the skills of the competitors. If so desired, a competitor can advance through Sportsman to Intermediate, Advanced and ultimately to the Unlimited category. As one moves up the categories, more advanced figures involving more complexity are added to the program. Also, as the competitor moves up the competition ladder, he's allowed to fly lower to the ground during his performance.

The competition resembles that of gymnastics or skating. There are three programs each pilot flies. The first is a Known program, a set of compulsory maneuvers (figures) that each contestant flies in the same sequence and in the same airspace as all the others. The second is the Freestyle. In this program the contestant combines numerous maneuvers and designs his own program. It's judged on degree of difficulty and level of execution. The final program, the one that usually determines the winner, is termed the Unknown. The night before this program the contestants are given a sequence they must fly. They can practice it mentally, but can't actually fly it until in competition the next day. Points are given for all three programs and added up to determine first, second and third place.

Aerobatics put enormous strains on the bodies of participants. G-forces, some up to levels experienced by fighter pilots, cause extreme physical strain. Under high G-forces, the blood has difficulty reaching the brain. It's not unusual for the pilot to experience a graying out of his vision. Eyesight becomes monochromatic as the eyes are starved of oxygen. If the forces continue, the pilot totally grays out and his vision is temporarily lost. Should the forces go beyond this level, the pilot blacks out and loses consciousness. Because of the physical strains of the sport, most pilots enter aerobatic competition in their twenties or thirties. Norm at age fifty was an anomaly and had a lot of catching up to do.

Norm considered aerobatics as, *"the pursuit of excellence with an airplane,"* and the best way to pursue that excellence was through competition. He set his goals high—the U.S. champion, United States National Aerobatic team and a chance to compete for the world championship. He said to himself, *"What are the obstacles to achieving my goal and which ones can I control."* He came to the conclusion that he needed the best machine suited for his task, and he needed the best training available.

It was time to put the trusty little Eagle in the hangar and move up to what most considered the best competition airplane in the world—the Edge 540.

Unlike the Christian Eagle, this airplane was produced in a factory and took eighteen months to manufacture. When it was delivered to him in 1998, Norm knew he had a plane with the power and maneuverability that could take him toward his goal.

Just as a world class skater, swimmer, tennis player or

golfer needs a coach, so too does a world class pilot. Norm sought out the best aerobatic coaches in the world. He pooled his resources with three or four other competitors and together they were able to hire coaches from around the world, to come to California and train them. The coach would be on the ground with a radio giving instructions to one pilot at a time, while the others listened in. This technique allowed the students to keep learning even when they weren't in the cockpit.

The coaching sessions went on for several days at a time and were termed camps by the participants. Initially Norm would organize six or seven camps a year and participate in ten to twelve contests a year. As his proficiency improved, he needed less coaching, but he continued to compete every month or two.

Norm spent a year in the Sportsman category, a year in Intermediate, two years in Advanced and finally reached the top category, Unlimited. In addition to the competitions, Norm started performing on the Air Show Circuit. Each year hundreds of organizations and airports sponsor shows, where the highlight is a performer or two who fly aerobatics for the hundreds of spectators on the ground. It was a great ego boost for Norm, but as a competitor he wasn't fond of it. Performers could make technical mistakes and the crowd would never know it; they were there to watch what they considered death defying feats, and the details went unnoticed. Performing made him a little sloppy and eventually Norm gave it up and concentrated one hundred percent on competition.

Norm devised a formula he calls, "*the rule of sixes,*" which describes the odds of making the U.S. Aerobatic team. *"There are six hundred thousand pilots in the United States. Six hundred of them compete in competition. Sixty compete at the unlimited level, and less than six men and six women make the squad."*

Each year five men and five women are selected for the U.S. Aerobatic team, based on their finish in the National championships. Those ten pilots compete against other countries and from those competitions, world champions are crowned. Over time Norm got very close. One year he finished eighth, once ninth and once tenth in the men's division.

One day when Norm and I were having coffee at the Sky Kitchen, I asked him, *"Are you disappointed getting so close and still not making the team?"*

Norm responded by letting me know that for him the destination was not nearly as important as the journey. *"I may never achieve the goal, but the pursuit alone is what has made it worthwhile. Along this road I've met people from around the world pursuing the same goal as I. I've met the best pilots from dozens of countries, and I'm able to call them my friends. The endeavor has given me more opportunities than I ever could have dreamed. I became the manager of the U.S. team, I'm president of the Unlimited Aerobatics Association, and I'm on the board of directors of the Experimental Aircraft Association. For the last fifteen years aerobatics has been my passion, and it continues to this day to be the most rewarding endeavor of my life."*

While munching on a burger, a pilot about the same age as Norm, leaned over, *"Hey, Norm, now that you're sixty years old, do you miss it?"*

"Miss what?" he replied.

"You know, that competition for guys without gray hair."

"Why would I miss it? The nationals are coming up this year, I'm gonna give it another go."

Norm flying right side up

Norm turning upside down

MAYOR OF THE SKY KITCHEN

Tales from the Sky Kitchen Cafe

MAYOR OF THE SKY KITCHEN

A pilot friend of mine in Chico, California recently took me into his hangar to show me a plane he had just purchased. It was a menacing looking bird, a bright yellow, fabric covered bi-plane used in the early 1940's to train Navy pilots. It had two open cockpits where helmets with earphones were needed for protection from the wind and for communication on the radios. Its huge radial type engine put out 450 horsepower. Two massive main wheels under the cockpit created the landing gear and a tiny wheel under the tail gave it ground mobility.

I said to my friend, *"John, who's going to teach you how to fly this beast?"*

He replied, *"Oh, I have this great guy who flew it up here, he can fly anything. You may know him. He's from San Carlos, his name is Butch."*

In 1951 the father of a twelve-year old boy traded a pistol from his gun making business for a bent up Piper Cub trainer. That simple transaction sparked the beginning of a glorious career in aviation for his son Butch, the future Mayor of the Sky Kitchen.

After Butch and his dad repaired the Cub, his father decided to get out of the gun business and into the aviation business. He leased a little airport with a dirt runway, rebuilt a couple more Cubs, and started a flying school. For eighty dollars he guaranteed a student would solo an airplane. Believe it or not, the flying school made money with those rates. Butch helped his dad make a profit rebuilding airplane engines, and at the same time he received an education in airplane mechanics.

Butch started flying lessons as soon as the business got started. He was a little guy, so his dad built extensions on the floor pedals to enable Butch to reach them. The regulations required a student to be sixteen to solo a plane; however, his dad let him go up by himself as long as he stayed close to home.

On his seventeenth birthday Butch passed the check ride for his license. When he was eighteen, he earned a commercial license and an airplane mechanic license; when he reached nineteen he added an instrument rating and a multi-engine rating.

By 1962, Butch was moving on with his life and joined the Army. When he arrived at Fort Benning in Georgia, the base flying club caught Butch's attention. He gave it a look and found it was a poorly run, underutilized facility. Butch managed to get an audience with the base commander and pitched an idea to him. *"The guys are getting paid once a month and blowing their money in the beer halls. How about we give them an alternative to use the money for flight instruction and they could end up with something constructive that would be useful for a lifetime?"*

The commander bought the idea and Butch was off to Atlanta, where he quickly qualified for a flight instructor license. When he returned to Fort Benning, he became the director, the flight instructor, and the mechanic for the club. He ran it all, and the club grew like crazy. Butch taught one hundred and eighty-five people to fly in two and half years. The army was great! The experience provided Butch with the opportunity to prove himself a great organizer as well as an able instructor.

Before he went into the army, Butch helped build and test fly a personal plane for a retired vice president of United Airlines. The man was very impressed with Butch's skills and said, *"If you ever think about flying for the airlines, give me a call. I'll write you a letter that will carry some weight, if you apply with United."* When Butch returned to the States, he called in the favor and included the letter in his application to United Airlines. He was hired on the spot, and at twenty-six, became one of the youngest pilots to be hired by a major airline.

The Boeing 727 was introduced to United Airlines six months after Butch was hired. He moved up to the 727 and flew it exclusively for twenty-five years, logging twenty-two-thousand hours before moving on to the Jumbo Jets. *"I spent more time with that airplane than I did with my wife."* In 1999 Butch turned sixty-years old, at that time the mandatory retirement age for airline pilots. From that day on Butch could be found every day having lunch at the Sky Kitchen.

He had already been holding court there for a dozen years, before I got into flying and discovered the center counter. He knew more about aviation than anyone I had ever met. He not only had flown hundreds of different makes and models, but he also built several planes and repaired dozens of others. When other local pilots had questions about flying or repairing their planes, they came to lunch at the center counter and had a consultation with Butch, the undisputed Mayor of the Sky Kitchen.

Butch played an important role in my life as a pilot. After I bought my first airplane, he became my mechanic. Several years after Len had his accident in the little 172, we bought a sleek Beechcraft Bonanza, and Butch taught us how to fly it. Len, our other partner Ron, and I would all pile into the airplane with Butch in the right seat instructor's position. With all of us aboard we could learn by each other's mistakes.

On the very first flight, I was in the left seat, Butch was in the right seat and Len and Ron were in two of the back seats. Our excitement was building as we accelerated down the runway for the first takeoff. Just as I pulled the plane off the ground, there was a popping noise and air was rushing in from the right side door. *"What happened?"* I managed to ask in an octave above my normal voice.

"Don't worry" Butch said calmly, *"Just come around and land; we're just fine."* The air noise was horrendous, but the plane handled normally and the landing was uneventful.

When we were on the ground Butch said, *"I purposely left the door unlatched. On this type of plane it will happen accidentally from time to time. I wanted you to experience it right now. When it happens the next time, you'll be at ease."* The door has popped on me at least a half dozen times, since that day—never again a big deal.

In the early 1980's the narcotics problems were beginning to erupt. Butch and a few other airline pilots, who hung around the Sky Kitchen would occasionally get a call from the local Sheriff's office. *"Hey Butch, could you take me up in your airplane around six tomorrow evening? I want to fly over Atherton and follow a guy to see where he goes. I think he's selling drugs."*

Over the next few years, the drug problem continued to escalate. A task force, combining local and federal agencies, was formed to fight it. The once random requests that Butch and the others received for missions started to become regular ones. Butch sat down with the task force and offered his organizational advice. *"You guys are wearing out our personal airplanes. You need to buy an airplane, and we'll figure out how to staff it with pilots for you."*

For years there had been a group of local Sky Kitchen pilots, who made up a Sheriff Air Squadron; however, they never had anything to do other than meet, share stories, coffee, and doughnuts. With the explosion of the drug problem, Butch realized that the existing squadron could be the nucleus for an all volunteer group of pilots who could fly the missions for the Narcotics Task Force. Butch and his group found an airplane, the task force paid for it, and more pilots were recruited to volunteer time flying it.

None of the pilots were law enforcement officers and none of them wanted to be. Every mission had at least three people in the plane. One was a sworn deputy, required by the county, who observed and acted as the authority to fly the mission. He ordered where to fly, who to follow, and took responsibility for the mission. The rest of the crew included the pilot in the left seat, and a co-pilot in the right seat, who acted as a spotter and radio operator. Hundreds of missions were flown with that protocol.

By 2010 the Sheriff Squadron had been assisting the drug task force for almost thirty years. The authorities were accustomed to having pilots and an airplane available and began using it for missions beyond drug enforcement, which included search and rescue, photography of crime sites, and criminal surveillance.

One morning Butch poured himself a cup of coffee and browsed through the morning paper. A story describing a local shooting caught his eye. The husband of the victim had told the police that his wife had committed suicide. Before Butch could finish the coffee, his cell phone rang. A police detective was on the line. *"Butch, could you assemble a team and meet me at the hangar?"*

"Ten o'clock," Butch replied and clicked off his cell.

Butch, and the co-pilot met the detective at the hangar and the story unfolded. Although the husband had told the police that his wife had committed suicide, ballistic tests had shown, that she was shot from a distance. The suicide was reclassified as a homicide and the police suspected the husband as the shooter.

The previous day the police attached a tracker to the husband's car, suspecting he was ready to flee. A tracker is a device, which can be attached to a vehicle and allows the police to follow and track the car to a destination. The detectives had been following the suspect, but had lost communication with the tracker in the hills that separate the Pacific Coast from the San Francisco Bay.

Detectives had followed the husband to a gated community, but the gates had closed before they could slip through without being seen. The detective asked Butch, *"Do you think we could find the gated community and maybe get a visual on the car from the air?" We know the suspect's at someone's house, but we don't know exactly which one. The last time we saw the car it was on Top of the Hill Road."*

Butch opened his computer and went to the Google Earth website. He typed in Top of the Hill Road and a cluster of houses jumped onto the screen. *"Do you recognize any of these houses?"*

The detective examined the screen. *"They all look the same from above."*

"No problem," Butch said, as he put a digital pin mark on the screen. Using the pin mark, Butch pulled up the coordinates for its location.

Butch loaded the coordinates into his GPS navigational unit in the airplane. The plane lifted off the runway at San Carlos and headed for the coordinates. Butch circled the pin mark for at least a half an hour, while the detective searched for a familiar landmark. *"Wait a minute, wait a minute, I see the gate that he drove through."*

Butch and the co-pilot looked down and sure enough, there it was. *"O.K. its time to start looking for your car."*

Below the plane sat huge palatial homes, some with ten car garages. Chances were the car was tucked away inside one of them. All of a sudden a house with a long driveway appeared out the window, and parked right in the driveway was the suspect's car. The co-pilot grabbed his camera and snapped a half a dozen pictures. Back at the hangar Butch opened up the Google Earth program for a second time. This time he matched the overhead photos to the overhead taken by Google. Once they had the house identified on Google Earth, they moved the pin mark. They had it; the exact address and the exact coordinates, where the car was parked. Butch jotted the address on a scrap of paper and handed it to the detective.

The following morning Butch poured his coffee, opened the morning paper, and read the headline. SUSPECT ARRESTED. Butch grinned and thought, *"I can't wait to tell this story at the Sky Kitchen."*

The mayor (right) seated at his favorite spot

OSHKOSH

Tales from the Sky Kitchen Cafe

Oshkosh

"*Hey, anybody want to go to Oshkosh?*" I'd been thinking about it for a long time before I put the question to the other ten guys at the center counter.

A young pilot who was new to the Sky Kitchen, looked up from his plate of fries, "*You talking to me?*"

"*I'm talking to whoever wants to go.*"

A flight instructor sitting next to me raised his eyebrows. "*You're not going to fly in?*"

"*Yea, why not?*" I responded a bit belligerently.

"*Mike it's a bitch to get into; there's airplanes everywhere, it's like a hornet's nest.*"

Ignoring the negative remark, my buddy Len piped up enthusiastically, "*I'll go!*"

Gordon, who had flown into Oshkosh once before with another pilot from the Sky Kitchen, took the last sip of his coffee and nodded his head, "*Count me in.*"

I had one last seat to fill. Encouraged by the responses, I looked up and down the counter for my last volunteer.

Helmut, an older pilot who lost his medical certificate and had to stop flying, sealed the deal. "*I'll be the fourth.*"

In 1953 a group of pilots who were interested in building aircraft at home and restoring vintage airplanes, formed an organization, the Experimental Aircraft Association (EAA). They started having annual fly-in conventions at various airports and by 1970 their event was attracting thousands of pilots, many of whom were not really interested in home-built airplanes, but were interested in the fly-in experience. To accommodate the large crowds that the event was attracting, the EAA moved it to Wittman Field in Oshkosh, Wisconsin.

Oshkosh had become more than a meeting place for the airplane homebuilders. It had become the Mecca for anyone interested in recreational aviation and aeronautics. The spectacle was extended from two days to a week long event, and it soon became the largest annual gathering of aviation enthusiasts in the world. Hundreds of exhibits sprung up in tents which were located around the field, and every day spectacular aerobatic shows and fly-bys took place in the skies overhead. Old and new aircraft were displayed, including military and commercial airplanes. Lectures were given in surrounding tents and musical entertainment was scattered around the property. For many pilots it was a social event where once a year they could renew acquaintances with other pilots who had become their Oshkosh Friends.

The event also began to attract the general public. People who previously had no experience with aviation bought tickets and crowds grew by the thousands. Huge lots were set up with bathrooms to accommodate the thousands of people who were camping under the wings of their planes, in tents, or in motor-homes. Hotels and motels in the surrounding area were sold out a year in advance. By 2009 the attendance soared to over 700,000 and over 10,000 planes flew into the field during the week of the event.

In 1998 the name of the event was changed from The EAA Convention and Fly-in to AirVenture Oshkosh; to the pilot community, it will always be referred to simply as Oshkosh.

In 1990 I bought an airplane that was classified as a Light Twin. It wasn't the same make as the one that Reid flew to Europe, but it was very similar in seating and in the power of the engines. By July of 1994 I had logged over five hundred hours in the twin. I decided it was time to make my pilgrimage to Oshkosh. That's when I threw out the challenge at the center counter.

The twin had an average ground speed of about two hundred miles an hour. Our route to Oshkosh would cover eighteen hundred miles, and simple math told me it would take at least nine hours of flying time. In addition to flight time we would need to make fuel stops which would add another couple hours to the trip. I decided that was too much for a single day; we planned an overnight stop on the way.

On the afternoon of July 28th I fueled the plane while the other guys loaded our gear. By 4 p.m. we left San Carlos behind and headed east on our first leg of the trip. Our plan was to fly non-stop to Rock Springs, Wyoming, but a red warning light on the instrument panel signaled a problem and I descended from 12,000 ft. to land in Battle Mountain, Nevada.

I taxied up to the local mechanic shop and shut down the engines. The mechanic opened up the cowl that covered the right engine and our hearts sunk as out dropped several ball bearings. Five heads squeezed in under the cowl and it was obvious to all of us that the alternator connected to the right engine had gone south.

In automobiles the electrical power to keep the engine running is supplied by the alternator, however, in airplanes the electrical power for the engine comes from another source. The alternator only supplies the power to run electrical instruments and radios. An airplane engine will run fine without an alternator. In addition to the obvious advantage of having two engines, a twin has an additional perk—two of every other piece of equipment. Our left engine alternator was operating perfectly. With a sigh of relief, we closed the cowl, fired up the engines, and were airborne only an hour behind schedule.

I had planned to land at Rock Springs before dusk, but our unexpected stop guaranteed that we would arrive after sunset. About 10 p.m. we spotted the runway lights against the pitch black background of the high desert. From afar it looked like a bright postage stamp pasted on a black envelope. The landing was uneventful and by ten-thirty we were eating dinner in the Holiday Inn next to a bar full of cowboys.

We woke early the next morning. Even before we took off from Rock Springs, I began to think about our approach into Oshkosh. I had read up on all the procedures. I knew it was going to be a chore to land at an airport that handles ten thousand planes in a week's time.

Before we took off I had Gordon jump into the co-pilot seat. He had flown into Oshkosh once before with another pilot from the Sky Kitchen and I knew I could use his help. Both engines fired up and we were airborne toward our last fuel stop, Mason City, Iowa. It was one of those humid Midwest summer days and a cloud cover was hanging at about twenty-five hundred feet. As we departed Iowa, I decided to fly the final two hundred and fifty miles into Oshkosh under the clouds. It made for a bumpy flight, but I wanted to be able to identify landmarks as we approached the field.

All of the air traffic control staff working the fly-in are professional full time controllers, managers, and supervisors employed by the FAA (Federal Aviation Administration). For this one week a year, they volunteer their services and set up a very well organized and structured system to control the air traffic in and out of Oshkosh and its neighboring airports. The air traffic controllers say working Oshkosh is their Super Bowl, and they compete to be picked as volunteers.

I had studied the procedures that needed to be followed for entrance to the airspace surrounding the event. Approaching from the west, we had to identify a set of coordinates that defined what was called Fisk Intersection. Fisk was the first location where controllers were stationed. In addition to the coordinates for the intersection, there was a tall flashing light, and a specific radio frequency to dial in.

We were ten miles west of Fisk Intersection, time to make our first communication. *"Oshkosh approach control, this is Baron seven, seven, seven, three, Romeo ten miles west of Fisk Intersection."*

"Baron seven three Romeo proceed to Fisk. When we ask for identification just rock your wings. From now on we'll talk to you but do not respond. Just comply with the instructions."

In less than five minutes we were over Fisk. The controller picked us up immediately through his binoculars. *"I see a Red, White and Blue Baron. If that is seven three Romeo, rock your wings."* I turned the control wheel quickly to the right and then to the left.

"O.K. Baron I've got you. The field is closed for the next thirty minutes for an air show. I'll need you to climb to fifteen hundred feet and fly a slow holding pattern behind the white Long-EZ aircraft just making a left turn in the pattern." Gordon identified the Long-EZ and we fell into line behind him.

A holding pattern is designed in the same shape as a horse racing track. In order to separate the planes, the slower ones were holding at a thousand feet while the faster ones were put into the pattern at fifteen hundred feet. We spent the next thirty minutes burning gas, following the plane in front of us, and getting ready for our final fifteen minute flight to Oshkosh.

Finally the radio came to life. *"O.K. everybody the field is open. We're going to peel off the faster planes from fifteen hundred followed by the slower ones at a thousand. Long-EZ you go first and the Baron will follow. We'll call the others out when it's their turn."* The Long-EZ pulled out of the holding pattern and I followed.

All of a sudden there it was! In the center of the field looking over the entire scene, stood the control tower which would handle several thousand take-offs and landings that day. There were two runways, a long one running north-south and a shorter one facing east-west. Huge fields were covered with parked airplanes, most of which had small tents or camping gear nearby. Parking lots were filled with cars, buses, and motor homes. A village area was near the hub of the action. It was overflowing with people strolling into large tents, buildings, and open air exhibits. There was a flight line of Warbirds; the combat planes from World War II. Near one of the runways were general aviation planes, some larger, some smaller than mine, all of which were being judged much like a Concours d'Elegance for automobiles. Off in the west corner were dozens of Ultra Light airplanes that looked like mosquitoes as they climbed to a hundred feet and landed back on the grass. I focused back on the plane in front of me.

"Long-EZ and Baron enter a right downwind for runway 36." The controller was directing us to enter the rectangular traffic pattern which would lead us after two more turns, toward our landing to the north. As we fell into line I glanced back through the side window. There were at least twenty planes following us in.

We were getting ready to make our base turn, the one just before our final turn to the runway. I went through our landing check list. Everything looked good. The landing gear was extended and we had flaps deployed. The airspeed was perfect for our approach to land. The controller was talking to everyone in the traffic pattern and all the pilots remained silent, doing their best to follow directions without opening their microphones.

The Long-EZ was making his turn to the final approach and I was starting my base turn, when all of a sudden out of nowhere, a four seat Piper Cherokee jumped in ahead of me.

"Gordon, where the hell did he come from?"

"I have no idea; he wasn't even in the line."

I didn't know what to do. I was instructed to maintain microphone silence and couldn't report the plane to the controller, but if I didn't turn right away, I would lose my sequence in the line and probably would not be able to land at all. Within ten seconds the controller was on it.

"Cherokee on base, where did you come from?"

"I've been here since Fisk," a confident voice answered back.

"No you haven't, now get out of the pattern and don't come back unless you wait your turn in line." The swagger was gone and the Cherokee wobbled out of line. As he disappeared, I swear it looked like the plane's nose was down and its tail was between its wheels.

I recovered my place in line and the controller surprised me with an instruction. *"Baron, we're landing two planes at a time. I want you to put yours on the first orange diamond. The plane behind you will fly overhead and land on the second diamond half way down the runway."*

I turned to Gordon, *"What's an orange diamond?"*

"I guess it's a landing marker at the front end of the runway."

I slowed the Baron way down. It wasn't a comfortable feeling. In a twin engine airplane a minimum speed is needed in the event of an engine emergency and I was approaching that speed.

"Come on Baron, you can slow that thing down more than that." I was getting close and the orange diamond was now visible.

"Come on Baron I know you can do it." I retarded the throttles all the way and the plane dropped with a thump onto the orange diamond.

The controller was back. *"Atta boy Baron, take the first taxi way on your left."* A bead of sweat dripped off my nose as I turned onto the taxiway.

A new controller came on the radio with a smile in his voice. *"Baron, good afternoon and welcome to Oshkosh."*

Aerial view Oshkosh 1994, the year we flew in

WWll Warbirds draw crowds

Tales from the Sky Kitchen Cafe

A RISKY BUSINESS

Tales from the Sky Kitchen Cafe

A Risky Business

By the age of fourteen Dave was an airport junkie. He was addicted to the sights, sounds, and smells of airplanes. It was like a drug; the more he tasted, the more he craved. While most kids his age were playing sports or listening to music after school, Dave was hanging out at the San Carlos airport.

The control tower hadn't yet been built; there were no restrictions to movement within its boundaries. Dave would ride his bicycle to the airport and wait for a car to drive in. When he spotted one, he jumped on his bike, rode across the middle of the runway, and waited on the other side for the pilot to get out of his car.

"Hi," said the red-haired teenager. *"Any chance I could wash your airplane today?"*

The reply was always the same, *"How much?"*

"I'll do it for a ride in your plane."

"Go find a hose; we're taking off in a half hour."

It didn't take long before Dave had a group of regulars. He'd wash their planes, run errands, and clean their hangars; anything to get a ride. If the pilots didn't need any chores done, they'd just say, *"Dave, just jump in the plane."*

By the time he was sixteen and eligible for a student license, Dave had flown in dozens of different airplanes.

Some kids are described as natural athletes or natural musicians, Dave was a natural pilot. Most students require a minimum of fifteen hours of instruction, before they are allowed to solo an airplane. Many take twenty or thirty, and some never qualify at all. Dave was allowed to solo in a record time of two hours.

Dave received his private license, when he was seventeen and his commercial and flight instructor licenses when he was eighteen. Flying came so easy for him that it hampered his ability to teach. He just couldn't understand why a student had such difficulty executing a maneuver which seemed so natural. Dave continued to give flight lessons, but couldn't make enough to support himself. He took any flying job he could get. He flew people, he flew packages, he towed gliders up in the air, gave aerobatic instruction and even gave skydiving lessons; he did anything that would get him up off the earth and pay him for it.

A couple of years passed. Dave knew most of the pilots on the field and made friends with a couple of guys who were building a homebuilt plane. They needed someone to test fly the plane and Dave volunteered. The plane was called a Quickie and it was the first of its kind to be built. It was tiny, had only one seat and only eighteen horsepower, but it was exhilarating. The Quickie was the first unconventional aircraft Dave had flown.

Years later, Dave was watching a radio controlled model airplane contest. He asked the operator of one of the planes, *"How many horsepower does your engine put out?"*

"Twenty," The operator responded.

"You know I've been up in the air in a plane, an actual airplane, that had only eighteen horsepower."

The guy looked at him as if he were nuts and walked

away. Dave smiled and thought, *"If I had had an engine as big as that model airplane, I would have made that Quickie go really fast."*

During the testing of the Quickie, Dave realized that he had another natural talent. He didn't have the engineering or mechanical experience which was needed for the construction of an airplane, but he could feel by flying it, if it needed changes. He could just feel it! The Quickie was the beginning of a new career in aviation for Dave—Test Pilot.

Dave knew that he couldn't be a flight instructor all his life and had been searching for a way to make his talents as a pilot profitable. He learned from his experience with the Quickie that he had an extraordinary ability to analyze what was wrong with an airplane, when he flew it; what he needed now was the ability to explain his analysis.

Building airplanes was about as easy as flying them. Along with a partner, Dave built his first airplane. Many others followed. After being involved in the actual building of a couple of airplanes, Dave was able to articulate his feel of the plane and the mechanical changes that were necessary to improve its flight characteristics; he could tell the builders, if the plane needed changes in the controls, the weight distribution or the power settings. If a system failed during testing, Dave could direct the builder to the parts that needed attention. The word slowly started to spread among the homebuilt airplane community. *"There's a guy in San Carlos who will fly the hell out your homebuilt and figure out what changes are needed before you get in it yourself."*

Early in his test pilot career, Dave had two incidents that would have made the average pilot look for a new line of work.

An airplane designer heard about the work Dave was doing, and hired him to test fly his prototype. It was a strange design; it was actually a sail plane (a glider), but it had a little rear engine that would allow it to launch itself without the use of another airplane to tow it into the sky. The initial tests were done by racing it down the runway to determine, if it had enough of a lift factor to start it flying.

The plane was engineered to lift off the runway at forty-five miles per hour, but Dave got it all the way up to sixty without any successful lift. He taxied back to the hangar and told the engineers that he had no elevator control, the input that's needed to raise the nose toward the sky. They tweaked the elevator a bit and sent him back for another run. This time, when he reached sixty the nose wheel hit a little reflector that was imbedded in the blacktop. The nose popped up and the plane was flying about six feet above the ground; the only problem was that Dave had no control over it. The plane came down on its nose, jumped back in the air, and came down again breaking it in half. Unfortunately for Dave, it also broke his back.

The second incident occurred about a year later, when Dave was test flying another exotic prototype. This plane essentially had three wings; the main wing in the center, a little wing on the nose, and the tail that acted as a wing. The engineers needed to know how slow the plane would fly before the wings would stall and the craft would quit flying. Dave took the airplane to 12,000 ft. and slowed it down. As predicted the plane went onto a stall and quit flying, but before he was able to react, the airplane began spinning toward the ground. Normally a spin would have been easy for Dave to recover from. In a normal spin the nose is pointing toward the ground and the plane is turning like a corkscrew as it descends. The plane makes a couple turns, before a recovery is easily made. Unfortunately, he was not in a normal spin; he was caught in a flat spin.

In a flat spin the nose doesn't point itself toward the

earth. The plane descends rapidly, spinning three-hundred and sixty degrees, while staying parallel to the earth. This is a much more difficult situation from which to recover. Dave began using recovery techniques but they resulted in the airplane turning upside down, putting him in an inverted flat spin. The plane was still doing 360's parallel to the ground, but his head was pointed toward the earth rather than the sky.

Dave looked at the altimeter; it read five thousand feet, not a safe enough altitude to keep playing with the controls. The plane was equipped with an attached parachute which could be used in an emergency. Dave deployed it. The plane turned right side up; when he looked up, he saw a tiny chute, not anything near the size he expected. The chute looked like the type he normally used just for himself, not for an airplane. He was right, the chute was way too small. The plane was descending too fast, and Dave knew was going to take a hard hit. He did some quick math and determined he had over two minutes before impact with the ground. He grabbed his clipboard, strapped it to his knee and printed on it in large letters: UNLESS I'M BURNING, DON'T TRY TO MOVE ME. He hit the ground, broke his back for the second time, and wasn't moved until the paramedics arrived.

By the time he recovered, Dave realized he had amassed twenty-five hundred hours flying Jets. He decided to make a try at getting hired by an airline. United Airlines was his choice, but most of the people being hired had a college degree and perfect vision. He had neither, and really didn't think he would be hired; consequently, he felt no pressure during the interview. He was relaxed and able to articulate his aviation knowledge without missing a beat. The test ride in the jet simulator went equally well, but Dave still felt he had no chance. A few weeks passed; a letter arrived with a class date to train as a flight engineer on the Boeing 747.

Dave brought the news to the center counter of the Sky Kitchen.

One of the guys at the end of the counter had to give his opinion. *"You'll never last,"* he barked.

Someone else chimed in. *"You're too much of a free spirit to fit into that mold."*

Dave laughed, *"Maybe so, but I'm going to give it a try."*

It turned out the counter was right. The job was boring. As an engineer he didn't get to fly. He sat at a little desk in the cockpit for sixteen hours at a time, monitoring instruments and managing the systems of the airplane. After awhile it felt as if he had an office job. Dave lasted a year and finally decided, *"This is absolutely not what I want to do the rest of my life."*

In 1984 the homebuilt airplane industry was revolutionized. An airplane designer, Lance Neibaur, expanded the use of composite carbon fiber, a material stronger and lighter than metal, by designing a plane that used it as its major component. In addition to its light weight, the Lancair, as it was named, was esthetically beautiful with its sleek lines and aerodynamic styling. The result of this design was a gorgeous, fast airplane. The planes were produced in kit form; sections of the plane were sent to the home builder in intervals; as one section was finished the next one would arrive. Thousands of Lancairs are now flying in countries all over the world. Several different models have emerged, with the newest posting a top speed of three hundred seventy miles per hour.

By this time Dave had gone back to test flying. The designer of the airplane in which Dave had broken his back (the first time) was doing design analysis for Lance's new airplane. He was well aware of Dave's ability to test and analyze aircraft and recommended him to be the test pilot for the Lancair. Dave test flew the initial prototype of the Lancair, and all the other models that were developed from it during the next ten years. He set multiple coast to coast and city to city speed records for airplanes of similar weight. He also was the first person to exceed 300 mph on a hundred mile closed course at the well known Sun and Fun Air Show in Florida.

In addition to test flying Dave had a habit of rescuing derelict homebuilt airplanes and normally, he paid nothing for them. The owners usually said, *"If you can fly it out of here, it's yours."* He found one such airplane at the San Jose airport. It was named the Mongster, and it was an old homebuilt which had won the Biplane championships at the famous Reno Air Races fifteen years earlier. Over the years the old champion had fallen from grace. It sat filthy with flat tires, its fabric skin ripped, and its engine rusty. Dave bought a dozen rolls of duct tape, patched it up and with his butt puckered to the seat, flew the ten miles back to San Carlos.

Dave was living in a garage at the time. He dismantled the plane and literally took it home and parked it in his bedroom. His intention was to rebuild it in the garage, but he got a call to fly fire bombers in Oregon and left before the restoration was even started. About two months later Dave received a call from Forbes, a friend who was into air racing.

"Hey Dave, what are you doing with the Mongster?"

Wondering why Forbes was interested, he replied,

"It's at home in the garage. Why?"

Forbes was getting excited. *"You know that airplane won at the Reno Air Races when they had a biplane class."*

Dave still didn't understand why Forbes was calling him. *"That was fifteen years ago."*

"They're bringing back the biplane class and they want your airplane to enter the race. It's on the 15th of September."

"I'm not interested; I'll be fighting fires until the end of September. Besides, it's in a million pieces."

Forbes could barely control himself. *"I'll make you a deal. I'll get a couple guys to help me rebuild it, and we'll take it to Reno for the races. If we win we'll split the prize money with you fifty-fifty."*

"Go for it." Dave replied as he hung up the phone.

The Mongster didn't win big prize money, but it took a respectable sixth place. Forbes called Dave. *"Hey Dave, there's a race down in Apple Valley next month; why don't you take a try at air racing."*

"I don't' think so. It looks boring just flying around in circles."

Forbes wouldn't take no for an answer. *"You should really try it. It's not as easy as it looks."*

Dave still wasn't convinced. *"I don't think so."*

Forbes used his ace in the hole. *"There's a neat trophy and if you place, the prize money will cover the gas."*

That piqued Dave's interest. *"O.K., I'll do it."*

Dave didn't win, but when he jumped out of the plane, he cupped his hands around his mouth and yelled over to Forbes. *"Damn that was fun. Where's the next race?"*

Air racing is the world's fastest motor sport. It resembles auto racing which takes place on an ovoid track, but the course is not marked by a roadway, it's marked by fifty foot poles called pylons. Depending on the speed of the airplanes in each class, the oval ranges from three miles to eight miles and the racers make multiple laps around the course. The day before each race the pilots make qualifying runs to determine their position at the start of the race. The fastest qualifier gets the pole position, or the inside position with the others line up abreast of him. The slower the qualifying time, the further to the outside the racer must start at the beginning of the race. The planes take off, assemble in a formation behind a pace plane and, when the signal is given, all eight pilots push their throttles to the maximum position and race full speed toward the first pylon; at speeds that often exceed 300 mph, the racers are flying wing tip to wing tip around the pylons trying to reach the finish line first.

The Granddaddy of air racing is the Reno Air Races. Every September at Stead Airfield in Reno, Nevada, the fastest racers in the country assemble for the Championships.

When Dave arrived for the first time in Reno, he felt like a rookie driver at the Indianapolis 500 auto race. Unlike the smaller races he had entered, this venue was huge. Each racer had a spot in the pits, where his crew prepared the plane and stood by for repairs. The grounds were covered with food and merchandise vendors along with exhibits for viewing. By the time the races got started the grandstands had filled with thousands of spectators, most of whom sported binoculars around their necks. For a rookie this was his first day in the major leagues.

Dave soon went from a rookie to a veteran. He participated every year and ended up competing in all five classes of racing offered at the Reno Air Races. With all the trophies he has received, one would think his most vivid memory would be from one of those races, but actually the day before the race in 1991 was his most exciting day at Reno. Dave was flying a Lancair, the same model for which he had been the test pilot during its design. He and his crew decided to run an experimental propeller on the plane, hoping to squeeze out a little extra performance.

Dave was at four thousand feet and started a dive toward the field to build up speed for his qualifying time. The plane accelerated quickly; when it reached a thousand feet, all hell broke loose. One of the blades separated from the experimental propeller and hurdled toward the ground. The engine was now out of balance and it started vibrating violently. The vibration started to tear the engine apart. Loose parts broke through the cowling (hood that covers the engine) and started bouncing off the windshield. Dave pulled the nose of the airplane skyward and was able to slow the plane enough to stop the propeller's, remaining blade, from spinning. The vibration stopped, when the propeller stopped. He pushed the nose of the plane toward the ground and gently glided to the field for a perfect landing.

The Lancair was out of the race. That afternoon Dave jumped into another plane which the crew had brought with them, and he took off for the qualifying run. Just as he had that morning, he climbed to four thousand feet, accelerated toward the field, and at a thousand feet it happened again; a blade separated from the propeller. By now he was an expert, and with nonchalance, shut down the engine, stopped the prop and glided back to land on the runway. It's not official, but Dave insists he holds the record for the most prop failures in a single day at the Reno Air Races.

Dave hadn't been back to the Sky Kitchen in several years, when he showed up for lunch. All the pilots at the center counter started to fire questions at him.

"Where the hell you been?" "Are you still testing airplanes?"

The counter went silent with disbelief when Dave replied. *"Well actually I'm test flying rockets."*

⬥

One of aviation's top test pilots, Dave has done first flights in 39 prototype aircraft. In 1998 the Society of Experimental Test Pilots honored him with the Spirit of Flight Award for his accomplishments in flight testing. Dave has set thirteen world speed records, eight of which stand. For fun and relaxation, he races his Formula V sports car at SCCA races and holds a track record at Infineon Raceway in Sonoma, Calif.

Dave has competed in more races (216) than anyone in the history of Reno Air Racing. In his twenty four years of racing Dave is the only pilot to compete in five classes; Biplane, Formula One, Sport, Unlimited, and Jet. He is a three-time Gold Champion in Sport Class ('98, '99, '00), Silver Sport Champion ('03, '04) and Unlimited Bronze Champion in '06. His fastest speed at Reno was <u>445 mph</u>.

———⊗⊗⊗———

As outlandish as his statement sounded at the center counter, Dave is actually test flying rocket airplanes. They are fueled by converting liquid oxygen and alcohol into a flame which produces thrust out the back of the engine. The planes are being built for a new event in air racing, The Rocket Racing League.

The name his friends gave him

The Mongster rescued from San Jose

The Lancair with only one prop blade and the cowl blown off

Reno air race. Dave (top) wing to wing at 300 mph

Reno air race. Dave (right) holding the lead.

Dave test flying a rocket plane.

FRIENDS AND FAMILY

Tales from the Sky Kitchen Cafe

FRIENDS AND FAMILY

Herb always wanted to be a pilot in the Air Corps, however, when he was called for service in World War II, a medical condition kept him from flying. Instead he was inducted into the Army. When the war ended in August of 1945, he was stationed in Tokyo and spent the next six months driving past Kempei Tai, the prison, where Hap had been incarcerated just a few months earlier. Of course, Herb didn't know that until fifty years later, when he met Hap during lunch at the Sky Kitchen and they shared their very different memories.

Herb's Japan was not Hap's Japan. The war was over; the civilians were relieved. Herb couldn't understand how these submissive and friendly people could have waged war against the world. They were completely the opposite of the brutal army that Hap had encountered. Later, however, Herb learned the truth how Japanese men were conscripted into service and who, through beatings, threats of death and even killings, were made into vicious fighters, who fought to their death.

Twenty-five years after the war, Herb realized his dream and earned his pilot license. At the same time, he discovered the Sky Kitchen and showed up regularly at the center counter. The friends he made there became the most valued of his life. He considers all of them as family.

I met Herb in 1978, and we often spoke over lunch about the risks and rewards of flying airplanes. We had a list of sayings that constantly crept onto our conversations.

About pilots who were always pushing the safety envelope, *"There are old pilots and there are bold pilots, but there are no old bold pilots."*

About pilots who flew into weather that was beyond their capabilities, *"I'd rather be down here wishing I was up there, than being up there and wishing I was down here."*

Warning each other about taking unnecessary chances, *"Never fly with anybody named Ace or Buzz."*

Reminding each other about landing with too much speed, *"Even if you have a long runway, it won't help, if most of it's behind the airplane."*

Emphasizing that all airplanes must be respected, *"The difference between a big airplane and a little one, is that the little one will kill you just a little."*

Our flying mistakes were a common conversation shared by Herb and others at the center counter. Being able to relate our mistakes to each other was our confessional, and it gave us relief to admit to them and still be able to have the approval of our peers. It also was post-graduate education for all of the participants, and many lessons were learned from the mistakes of others.

Having the knowledge and ability to fly an airplane and being able to navigate it, often through clouds, rain, and darkness is an incredibly rewarding experience; it is, however, a very unforgiving endeavor. All of us have made mistakes piloting airplanes, and most of us have been lucky enough to survive them. Some have not been so lucky and often a small mistake or a second of poor judgment has been enough to permanently remove one of our comrades from the Sky Kitchen.

One such incident occurred, while Herb was having his usual lunch at the center counter. The large windows allow a good view of the runway and Herb casually watched as Bob's big twin engine Queen Air took off. Suddenly the sound of the engines permeated Herb's ears. *"Something doesn't sound right. One of those engines is making an awful noise."* Herb and a couple other pilots jumped off their stools and went to the outside deck.

Bob was what most pilots would consider to be an old, bold pilot. At ninety-one years old, he had survived fifty missions in a B17 bomber over Europe, and had survived several crash landings in two or three of his own airplanes during his next sixty-five years of flying. It appeared that he had avoided the fate of the old bold pilot theory, but as Herb watched, the theorem was proven once again.

The Queen Air was at only six hundred feet when it banked to the right, stalled, and went straight down into the waterway beneath it. Bob, another experienced pilot Bill, and a backseat passenger were all killed.

No one will ever know who was making the decisions in the Queen Air, Bob or Bill, but it really doesn't matter; two of Herb's family members will not be having lunch again at the Sky Kitchen Cafe.

Twenty-five years ago Herb decided to create a permanent chronicle of the Sky Kitchen family. He came up with the idea to write a short profile of each member, and asked if I would be the test case. He condensed my story down to two and half pages, and it turned out great. That was the start of Herb's journey to create a permanent record of The Family: Pilots, airport employees, and owners of businesses at the airport.

The project became huge. Herb has spent thousands of hours over the past twenty-five years talking to his friends, collecting material and writing their profiles. To date, he has written over five hundred, filling seven telephone book sized volumes. The project has been his labor of love, but it has not been without sadness. Since he began his work, thirty-five of his friends have passed away, some of them in airplane accidents like Bob and Bill.

Because of his biographical work, Herb has had a personal connection with every regular at the Sky Kitchen. He willingly helped organize the memorial for his friends, Bob and Bill. It reminded him once again that with the joy of meeting new friends at the center counter, also brings great sorrow, when they are lost.

However, Herb doesn't let the sad days get him down. He always remains cheerful and optimistic, looking forward to the next new face, new friend, and new family member at the center counter. When he spots one, he thrusts out his hand and says, *"Hi, I'm Herb, this seat taken?"*

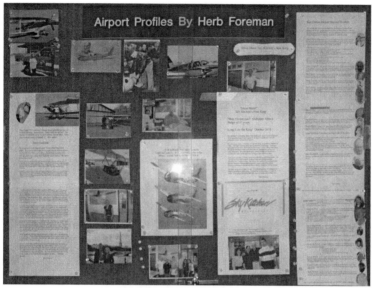

Herb's work on display

Herb (center)

Friends at the center counter

Friends at the center counter

Tales from the Sky Kitchen Cafe

THE AMERICAN DREAM

Tales from the Sky Kitchen Cafe

THE AMERICAN DREAM

In 1968 a developer built a new terminal building at the San Carlos Airport. It was an ambitious project. He provided space for a lobby, restrooms, an airport administration office, a flight school, an insurance agency, a pilot store and a small restaurant that the new owner named Andy's Coffee Shop.

Andy had high hopes for his little coffee shop, but after a year he couldn't turn a profit and walked away from the business. A mother and her two daughters took it over and renamed it the Sky Kitchen Cafe. They worked hard, but they too couldn't make the business profitable, and after two years, it was sold again. The new owner only spent eleven months in the restaurant before she also walked away. It appeared to the developer that the airport was not a suitable place for a restaurant.

In the nineteen-fifties a fourteen year old boy named Bahram was growing up in Iran, which at that time had a very good diplomatic relationship with the United States. President Eisenhower and later President Kennedy were heroes to the Iranians and were given huge parades whenever they visited. Bahram dreamed of visiting America. He soaked up news and magazine articles about America; he went to see American made movies whenever he had the chance.

The movies set the dream in motion for Bahram. Many of them depicted a laid back American lifestyle, using California as their backdrop. There were Elvis movies, Beach Boy movies, scenes from Los Angeles and scenes from San Francisco. The one that stuck in Bahram's memory was that of a young man driving in a convertible over the Golden Gate Bridge with San Francisco in the background. That vision became America for him.

The same year that Andy's Coffee Shop opened in 1968, Bahram turned twenty-six, and the dream of going to America still burned inside him. He mustered the courage to chase his dream. By the end of the year he had said goodbye to his family, his friends, and his homeland and made the journey to America as had so many hopeful immigrants before him.

He had relatives in the United States, but he arrived with very little money, no job, and no command of the English language. He soon found that people in America questioned his strange sounding Middle-Eastern name that they couldn't pronounce. He decided to trade it for an American one. Bahram became Ben.

Ben had a cousin in Berkeley, a university town on the east side of the San Francisco Bay. His cousin found him a job as a dishwasher in a local restaurant. Ben had an extraordinary work ethic, an attribute that would lead to his eventual success. He took his mediocre job seriously and still laughs at being told:

"You are the best dishwasher this restaurant ever had!"

Ben washed dishes all day and in order to learn English went to adult school at night. It took awhile for him to feel confident enough to converse in English, however, by the end of 1969 he was communicating in a language that eighteen months earlier had been totally foreign to him. Like most who learn English as a second language, he still speaks with a slight accent. For Ben it's a source of pride when he says, *"with every accent is a culture left behind."*

The next five years were spent getting on the job education in the restaurant business. Ben was promoted from a dishwasher to a cook where he was able to observe closely what made a restaurant a success rather than a failure. Later he was offered a job as a bartender in a restaurant on the west side of the Bay near San Carlos. It was there that he got wind of a small restaurant that was for sale at the San Carlos Airport, the Sky Kitchen Cafe.

The developer was ecstatic when he learned that he might have a buyer for the little coffee shop which he had written off as a total loss. Ben wasn't naïve. He knew the business had already failed under three separate owners, but he was confident that he could make it work. He didn't have much money, however, he was able to talk the seller into financing the purchase and they negotiated a contract. In 1973 he became the fourth owner of the Sky Kitchen Cafe.

Reviving a dying business wasn't easy! The three failures of the coffee shop during the last five years had put a dark cloud over the business. The local pilots avoided the restaurant, and a mere change in ownership was not a good enough reason for them to start eating there. Ben had to prove himself and his food to the local pilots.

The first two years were brutal. A few relatives helped as waitresses, but Ben did everything else. He was doing the cooking, washing, mopping, accounting, bookkeeping, depositing, and marketing all by himself. He often came to work before dawn and left after the sun had set.

Ben knew he had to bring the local pilots back into the coffee shop. He did it with quality food, fair prices, and the great work ethic he brought with him from his previous jobs. Slowly the pilots started to drift into the Sky Kitchen. Finally, after two years, the word had gotten around; a base clientele of pilots were ordering fifty to sixty breakfasts and lunches a day. Ben was pleased, but at an average of $1.80 per meal, he was barely paying his rent.

The turning point for the Sky Kitchen came when the non-pilot population discovered the coffee shop and spread its reputation by word of mouth.

"You have to try that coffee shop at the airport."

"Have you had the lunch at the airport?"

"Try that Sky Kitchen for Sunday breakfast."

People who worked in the area started to trickle in for lunch, and families started to fill the tables on the weekends. The kids loved the window seats where they could see the airplanes take-off and land. All of sudden Ben was serving a hundred fifty to two hundred meals a day.

There were no formal regulations; however an order of seating had developed. The pilots gravitated to the center counter, and the other customers usually chose the tables around the sides or in front of the windows. Occasionally non-pilots found themselves at the center counter in the midst of pilot talk. They often came back just to listen to the flying chatter that took place there. The pilots themselves had become a drawing card for other customers.

By 1978 Ben was making a good living. It was then that he was introduced to a young eighteen-year old woman who had just come to America from Iran. Ben and Zohreh were married within a year, choosing to hold their reception at the prestigious Villa Hotel. It was an upscale place where celebrities, entertainers, wealthy businessmen, and other visitors to the San Francisco Peninsula would often stay. The couple had their picture taken on a balcony that was situated over the well known Villa Coffee Shop. Thirty years later in 2009 Ben and Zohreh owned that restaurant.

Originally, Ben thought the Sky Kitchen would be a temporary career stop, where after a couple years, he would move on to other ventures. His thinking changed when he realized how supportive and non-judgmental the pilots were toward him. He loved the pilots who came to the Sky Kitchen day after day to meet at the center counter. In 1980 the pilots proved their loyalty to him once again.

On November 4th 1979, a diplomatic crisis took place between Iran and the United States. A group of Islamic students and militants took over the United States Embassy in Tehran as a gesture of support for the Iranian revolution. Fifty-two US citizens were held hostage for four hundred and forty-four days until January 20th 1981.

Many Iranian born businessmen in the United States were the targets of discrimination. Bricks came through store windows and boycotting of businesses was not unusual. Ben was nervous. Would this international crisis become his crisis? Would his customers blame him? Would they keep patronizing his coffee shop? His fears were unfounded! Not a single pilot stopped eating at the coffee shop. Nobody blamed Ben for the chaos taking place in Iran, and it was still hard to get a seat at the center counter.

By 1990 the success of the Sky Kitchen allowed Ben to invest in two more restaurants—a breakfast fare in an old train depot, and a take-out-only with a delivery service. He utilized the same formula he had employed at the Sky Kitchen—good food, fair prices and hard work. Ben eventually sold those restaurants only to replace them with two more, one of which was the coffee shop at the Villa Hotel. Throughout this time he held on to his flagship, the Sky Kitchen Cafe.

I shared thousands of lunches with other pilots at the center counter. I was accustomed to seeing Ben in the kitchen directing traffic or unloading supplies. In October, 2010 I stopped in for some lunch and conversation. Ben wasn't in the kitchen. He was having a cup of coffee at the center counter, laughing and joking with a group of pilots who had been his customers for years.

After working seven days a week for thirty-seven years at the Sky Kitchen, Ben had finally sold it. Back in the kitchen were the new owners, two young guys working with the energy that Ben had possessed back in 1973. I grabbed a cup of coffee and sat down next to Ben. We talked about old times and then he got up and started toward the door.

"Hey Doc, you wanna take a ride?"

"Sure" I replied.

We walked to the parking lot, and Ben opened the door of a new silver roadster convertible. I got in. He drove out of the parking lot and jumped on the freeway going north. We were silent as he played with the GPS. As I glanced over to check our destination a smile came over Ben's face… he had achieved his American dream. He punched in:

G-O-L-D-E-N-G-A-T-E B-R-I-D-G-E

Epilogue

Tales from the Sky Kitchen Cafe

Epilogue

In 1998 after twenty years of lunches at the Sky Kitchen, I retired, and along with my wife Bev, moved two hundred miles north to watch our grandchildren grow up. I'm not the only fraternity member, who is missing lunch there these days. Jim Baldwin, my instructor went on to become a 747 Captain and in four years will retire from Northwest Airlines. Phil Webster retired to Sacramento and is writing a book of his memoirs. Hap Halloran still lives in the Bay Area, but can no longer make the drive to the Sky Kitchen. Len Vinci retired to Arizona and maintains his pilot license. Gordon Cerrudo, a companion on the Oshkosh trip lives near Len in Arizona and flies his plane regularly back to San Carlos. Helmut Fenski, another companion on the Oshkosh trip lost his wife of sixty years. He died soon after of a broken heart.

Unbelievably most of the pilots, who sat at the center counter thirty years ago, still come regularly to lunch at the Sky Kitchen. Syl Heumann parks his Ferrari in the disabled spot right in front of the restaurant. Butch Pfeifer still holds court at the center counter. Norm DeWitt remains determined to make the U.S. team. Reid Dennis is semi-retired and often flies the Albatross that took him around the world. Jeanne

McElhatton teaches her Fear of Flying Clinic every six months instead of every three. Dave Morss continues to test and race airplanes and Dave Forbes, who got Dave Morss interested in racing, is a retired airline pilot, who is seen regularly at the center counter. Herb Foreman never misses a day with his Sky Kitchen family, and Ben and Zohreh Abolmoluki are now customers, not owners.

Since 1978 I have logged over thirty-five hundred hours in the cockpit, and I still own an airplane in partnership with a retired airline pilot. It's getting harder to hold onto my medical certificate, but somehow I've managed to pass the exam every year. Along with the old timers at the Sky Kitchen, there are new pilots, who bring their own stories to the counter. About once a month I make the one hour flight back to my old airport in San Carlos, where I take a seat at the center counter, and listen to new *Tales from the Sky Kitchen Cafe*.

My sincere gratitude

To all the subjects of my stories, Len Vinci, Jim Baldwin, Phil Webster, Hap Halloran, Syl Heumann, Reid Dennis, Jeanne McElhatton, Norm DeWitt, Butch Pfeifer, Dave Morss, Herb Foreman, Ben & Zohreh Abolmoluki, for the many hours they spent in interviews, checking facts, and donating photos from their personal collections.

To Jim Baldwin for allowing me to use segments of a story entitled *Rookies and Checkerboards*, written by him for *Contrails*, a quarterly publication.

To Dick Knapinski and the Experimental Aircraft Association for their donation of photographs taken at the Oshkosh Air Venture.

To Keith Matteri for allowing me to use photos taken by his father, Lawrence E. Matteri, while serving during World War II in the Pacific theatre.

To Walter J. Boyne for taking the time from his busy schedule to review the book and write such an inspiring foreword.

Mike Paull practiced dentistry in San Carlos, California for thirty-five years, until 1998. He earned his private pilot license in 1979 and followed with an instrument rating, commercial license, multi-engine rating and a flight instructor license. He has compiled thirty-five hundred hours of flying time. Mike and his wife Bev are retired and now live in Chico, California.

Ordering Information

www.skyhawkpublishing.com
or
www.amazon.com
www.barnesandnoble.com

For direct purchase
Mail your book order to:

Skyhawk Publishing
3173 Canyon Oaks Terrace
Chico, Ca. 95928

Make checks or money orders payable to Skyhawk Publishing

$14.95 plus

Shipping charges, add $3.00 for first book and $1.50 each
additional book. All orders shipped Special Fourth Class Mail
(Bookrate)

California destinations, add 8.25% sales tax, ($1.23 per book)

E-mail: Skyhawkpub@aol.com

9 780615 441092